No More Crumbs: How to Stop Dating (and Mating) for Crumbs and Get the Cake You Deserve in 10 Crucial Steps!

Samantha A. Gregory

DEDICATION

This book is dedicated to my daughter Alexzundra, one of many hopeful young ladies waiting to experience love.

This book is also dedicated to the numerous women who have, unfortunately, experienced the crumbs. I have been there, done that, and gotten the t-shirt. That little thing is all in tatters and yours may be too, but there is hope and a better way. At the end of this journey of relationship knowledge and unveiling of the truth you will stand victorious...eating cake!

CONTENTS

ACKNOWLEDGMENTS

Writing this book has been a labor of love. In my mind it has taken forever to get it done, but actually it only took a few months. Fortunately, self-publishing makes it easier to get books to press much faster.

I want to thank my parents, Samuel and Brenda Gregory for birthing and raising me to be a lady and a thinker. That can be a deadly combination for most men, but I've learned to use my powers for good.

Thank you to my siblings, Samuel Gregory, Jr. and Samala Gregory Carrington for your encouragement and love. I think we must be the closest siblings in the world. I still can't understand how other siblings can fight and hate each other. You both are my first best friends and I love you.

Thanks to my best friend Meredith Stewart. You are an inspiration to me and your life is a testimony that no matter what hell you have been through you can still make your dreams come true. You are my BFF for life!!!

The ladies of Buckhead Community Fellowship are phenomenal. Without your encouragement and hunger for this book I don't think I would have gotten it out this quickly. You drove me to write and get it out there into the world. Thank you Rhonda Maddox, Wendy Jamerson, Marjorie Douglas, Shirlynn Evans, Shante McClendon , Heidi Day-Jessup, Wendy Roberson, Aleta Saunders, Geogina Tsikiwa, Brynda Cadogen. I can't forget the men of BCF. Special thanks to Calvin Roberson and Tom Jessup. I appreciate your encouragement, conversations, and example of manhood.

I had several contributors for this book. They bravely shared their stories to expose the truth about crumb. They showed what it looks like and feels like. They tell the truth so the women reading this book will know what a crummy relationship looks like. You deserve special acknowledgements for your contribution and bravery. I wish I could give you all a medal of honor.

A Special Thank You to:

Jen Hancock
Writer, Speaker, Humanist

Vondie Lozano, MFT, Ph.D.
Licensed Marriage & Family Therapist
Relationship Expert
http://vondieslovechats.com/my-story

D.B.
Bold Selah, LLC
www.Boldlioness.com

Stella Vance
Dancing with Duality: Confessions of a Free *Spirit*

Leah
TheMiracleJournal.com

L. Writes
"My Heart Speaks..."
http://www.Lariewrites.com

L. Carroll
Lady L. Media
http://www.ladylmedia.com

Krishunna Pearson
The Making Of A Lady
www.makingalady.org

Rhonda Sciortino
Author, Succeed Because of What You've Been Through.
http://www.rhondasciortino.com

Stephania Vereen - Author, Speaker, Blogger
www.stephaniavereen.com

Elaine Purnell
Author of The Mistress

Preface

MY STORY

I grew up in the 70s at the tail end of the women's liberation movement. At the tail end of the bra burning and women declaring they could roar just as loudly as the men. I grew up after the Vietnam War and at the beginning of the Cold War. I was oblivious to both but very familiar with the residual effects of these events.

The women in my family were strong-willed, domineering, and often misguided by what they saw in the media. They thought they had to be hard, tough, and many times rude. They did not see the good in men or even see them as people most of the time.

What I didn't learn until much later was that most of the women in my family had been raped, molested, or abused in some way by men. Their defense was to be strong-willed, domineering, and misguided. They taught their daughters, my mother and aunts, how to be this way too, or at least not to be too afraid to question things.

I came along, and though my family was intact, it was in disrepair. I was sermonized and lectured about the evils of boys and men. I had this uncanny fear of them, except my father, of course. I was told to keep my legs closed and the books open. I was scolded if a boy liked me. I was never told I was pretty so I spent most of my life trying to prove I was at least smart. Pretty was for my sister, who is high yellow, has hazel colored eyes, and light brown hair. I was and am the opposite with my darker skin and brown eyes. But because I was perceived as smarter that even caused a bit of friction. But I loved (and still love) my sister and protected her with my life.

I was a classic case of surrogate mother to my siblings because I was the oldest. I sacrificed a carefree life because I was the oldest. I felt this pressure early on and didn't think I had a choice. They were my responsibility from the time we got up to the time my parents got home in the evening. It's taken me awhile to get over that feeling and let them live their lives without me rescuing them, but I digress.

By the time I was a teen I was angry and hurting because I felt neglected and used. My mom suffered acute and chronic depression after we moved to another state. She was verbally abusive and negligent. My dad was a workaholic and withdrawn much of the time. They had a volatile relationship and my grandmother fueled the fire with her nagging and rudeness. She interfered and disrespected my parents and their marriage.

Having never really grown up, my mother was like a woman-child in need of the father that left when she was very young. She wanted my dad to fill the void but it was not something he was equipped to do. She resented them both and made life hard for the family and for herself. My grandmother had her in a grip of guilt from the day she was born. Unfortunately she treated my mother liked dirt, but my mom kept going back for more in hopes of receiving a little love this time around. It never materialized.

Seeing all of this did quite a number on my psyche. I got the message that I was not enough, not worthy of attention; which all translated to "not lovable." I was clothed, fed, and given a place to lay my head. I went to school and was later homeschooled. I went to church and had friends to hang out with on the weekends, but day in and day out I felt invisible. I was longing to hear the words "I love you" and "You matter." I didn't, so in essence I was set up to accept crumbs in life because that was all I received growing up.

On the outside we looked like the perfect family to all the church folk. My siblings and I were well-behaved, talented, and fun to be around. People sought us out and wanted to come to our house. As time went on, I became angrier and quite a no-nonsense person. I did not take BS from anyone, especially boys. I was taught they only wanted to use girls, but at the same time I craved their attention.

I was taught that it was sinful to have sex before marriage so I saved myself for the man I would marry. I gave guys a hard time when they tried to talk to me thinking they would leave me alone, but ironically they became more persistent.

I had boyfriends starting at age 14 or 15. A guy sent a message saying he liked me and eventually we started talking. This happened only on the weekend because that was the only time I saw guys from church. If there was a revival I got to see my friends and guys every night. My first kiss was from a guy that was from a notoriously wild and broken family. He was cute though and was my friend's cousin. He was a little too advanced for me, so I broke up with him.

I had very clear boundaries at that age but I let them

slowly fall as I got older because I desperately wanted to be loved. I had other boyfriends, I kissed them, I went to the edge but I would never have intercourse because I was saving myself for marriage. My boyfriends treated me well but if I saw any sign of misbehavior, rudeness, or abusiveness I wouldn't give a guy the time of day. He was blacklisted and I went on being me... until I got into my 20s.

The message I had in my youth stuck with me until I got into my 20s. I had gone to college after high school and graduated with an Associate's degree. I was planning to become an Architect but I did not know how to move on after the pre-architecture program. I was the first to go to college in my family so I was feeling my way through the process. My parents didn't or couldn't help me navigate through and I didn't have any mentors to help me either.

So I came home with much dread. I threw myself into church work; leading the youth group, being the treasurer, and teaching bible class. I was an usher and board member all at the young age of 21 and 22. I felt intense loneliness and depression. There were no guys to really date at my church and I did not visit other churches often. Dating guys who were not of my faith was out of the question.

My best friend, sister, and I would hang out at my apartment and talk about what we wanted in marriage. We talked about what it would be like to have sex and about how exciting we wanted it to be. We talked about the fact that there were no men around worth dating and tried to deal with our issues as best we could. The men that were in our church were married, old, or lame and that certainly didn't help us out. We were the blind leading the blind.

One day at church I saw a very tall man at church. I thought he was attractive but did not give him much thought because I was sure he wouldn't have given me much thought. I didn't know he was watching me and asking around about me. Later on he approached me in a mysterious kind of way. It was enough to peak my curiosity so I asked about him.

My dad knew of him and a bit of his background. He had two children and wasn't married to the mother. He asked me on a date and when I told my dad he said, "You want to date a man with kids?" I didn't know what to say to that. It had been my policy to never date a man with kids because I didn't want to deal with baby mama drama. But I was desperate for attention at that time so I threw that policy out the window. My dad's response didn't help matters.

So I began dating this very tall, very handsome guy and he showed me a side of life I had never experience. He spoiled me, gave me attention, talked and laughed with me. He respected that I did not want to have sex before marriage at the time. He took me on motorcycle rides, to the park and other out of the way places. He never tried anything with me that I didn't want to do.

He cooked for me, rubbed my feet, brought me food when I was at work, and played the saxophone for me. He and I argued and made up. He accepted me and didn't seem to expect anything from me. He was a gentleman. He opened doors and got upset when I forgot to let him. He took care of me. Then things got complicated.

His baby mama started refusing to let him see his children. He got desperate and neglectful. His job took him away for long periods so I didn't hear from him. I was needy and afraid of losing him so I got careless.

We talked about getting married but he made all kinds of excuses and flippant comments about it just being a piece of paper. I wouldn't budge on the issues and like a silly little fool

I debated with him. It was a no-win situation. Eventually he agreed and we began planning a wedding. But something was not right; I just didn't see the signs.

I moved in with him and eventually we started having sex. Really good sex. Mind-blowing sex. Sex with him was like chocolate, a foot massage, and an explosion at the end. He was very skilled and very generous. He took care of me and I never had to wonder, "Is this all?" I never had any frustration about sex and was sad for other women who settled for less than an experience like I was having everyday sometimes two and three times a day.

But it didn't last because my good girl guilt was nagging me. Everything was perfect except we were not married and his baby mama was causing him to be stressed. My guilt and his distraction were a deadly combination. Things were about to explode and end badly. I could not communicate my fears and concerns to him because I had never seen a healthy relationship where talking to each other and conveying feelings in a healthy way was normal. I was stunted in that area and so was he. My fears came out as anger and desperation (there's that word again). I pushed and pulled, I tried to force things and when they didn't go my way I left.

I could not resist him because we bonded sexually and emotionally. The bond was so deep, so strong that neither of us could resist even after he married his baby mama a few months after we broke up under threats he would never see his children again. When I found out I was livid, heartbroken, and in despair. I left town to get away. I was angry that he didn't fight for us. I wanted to kill him because he hurt me so badly. He admitted the marriage was a mistake but he thought he was doing the best thing for everyone. That didn't compute with me. I was the one he said he loved and would never leave. I promised him that I would never leave him when he asked me. We were supposed to be together forever.

While I was away he called me almost every day. He told me he missed me and was miserable without me. He told me he didn't love her or want to be with her but wanted me. I was sucked back in because I missed him too and needed him.

I went back home using some excuse about not being able to find a job. I lived with my parents for a while then got my own place after I found a job. That new place was where I conceived my daughter. The dumbest part of all of this was that neither of us used birth control. I had many spontaneous abortions because I was late many times. When I did have my period, it was a lot more than "normal." I counted myself blessed but I was too dumb to take precautions.

During the affair I felt guilty and he tried to assuage my guilt with gifts and reassurance. He was in the process of getting a divorce, which was proof to me that he was serious about wanting to be with me. But I learned, by "accident," that he had gotten his wife pregnant. I was two months pregnant when the baby was born. I had really fallen far away from the message of my youth. I was lost in a sea of crumbs and could see no way out.

My baby was born healthy and beautiful. I was in the throes of post-partum depression and I hated my baby daddy. He was there during my last hour of labor when, after 21 hours, he showed up and it was decided I should have a C-section.

Throughout this book I will share stories of women, smart women, who found themselves caught up in toxic relationships. Most woke up from the nightmare and others are still finding their way out. These stories are meant to show you the signs and symptoms of toxic, crummy relationships. They are meant to show it can happen to anyone and to show that you can get out and choose healthy relationships.

I am college educated, in my 40s now. I was involved about 10ish years ago with a psychotic individual who turned into a stalker when I left. Well, actually he left, and then became a stalker, which just shows you how incredibly psychotic the situation I was in was. It was incredibly toxic. It took me almost a year to extract myself from a 4 month long distance romance. It took me another year to admit I was being stalked. I had to get the FBI involved, it was horrid. When my boyfriend (now husband) first started to complement me, I cried, I couldn't handle someone being nice to me. I had to relearn how to be in a healthy relationship. It is really amazing just how much your sense of self can be manipulated by someone and how harmful it really is.

When I talk about this to other people, I tell them, the best thing that came out of this for me was to realize, it can happen to anyone. It isn't just stupid girls who end up in toxic relationships. If it happened to me, and I am clearly a don't-take-crap-from-anyone sort of girl, it can happen to anyone. This guy reeled me in like a fish on a hook and I was completely incapable of defending myself emotionally. Intellectually, I was able to extract myself, but it was REALLY hard to do. I did it, but it was about the hardest thing I have ever done. And considering I have lost a child, that's saying a lot.

Jen Hancock
Writer, Speaker, Humanist

Samantha A. Gregory

1 LOST IN A SEA OF CRUMBS

A couple of years ago I attended a retreat with a group of ladies from my church. Like typical women do, we talked about everything under the sun. Eventually, the topic fell on relationships and specifically singles' relationships. It was tragic really because the women were absolutely beautiful and talented and spiritual. The question that came up time and again was "why do we accept the crumbs men throw at us?" Why do we fall for men that neglect, abuse, cheat, and play us? How can beautiful, educated, financially successful women fall for men like these over and over again?

They say they love us and then ignore us. They give us their undivided attention for a few weeks or months then disappear all together. They lavish us with sweet words then suddenly it seems they have nothing to say. We have to almost beg for a conversation. It seems the person we love the most cherishes us the least. IThe relationship always starts out perfectly doesn't it. My relationship was no different. Here is a bit of my story.

The man was an Adonis-like specimen for me. He was over six feet tall, well-built, pensive, and intelligent. I was shocked he noticed me. We went out a couple of times and soon were inseparable. He said the nicest things to me and made the butterflies in my stomach dip and soar. We were getting serious and talking about the future and being together. Everything seemed perfect until we had sex. He was my first because I wanted to wait until I got married. He became too irresistible so I gave him my most precious possession.

He was addictive and the more I tried to resist the more I gave in. Soon guilt and religious torture were my constant companions. I worried about sending us both to hell because I felt like I was tempting him to want me so much and could not resist. We broke up and got back together a million times, it seemed like, because he would not marry me and I could not live with the guilt.

Finally during one of our breakups, around the holidays he married someone else. I was devastated and horrified because all that time he said he loved me!

I moved away to get myself together. He called me everyday telling me his regrets and wishing he had not gotten married but that it was the best decision for most people involved, including the children he had with the woman he married.

So my life was a case study. Would I cave and give in to his insanity plea or would I walk away?

What makes a woman, a smart, educated, beautiful woman, get on bended knee to eat the crumbs a man drops from his table? What makes a woman accept neglect, broken promises, and all forms of abuse for the attention of a man? Are his physical prowess, smooth words, and electric touch so good it would cause her to lose all reason?

It seems every day millions of women dive, crawl, and lie prostrate under the tables of the men who say they love and eat the crumbs of deceit, invisibility and misery each and every day. They know the situation is not right. It does not feel right. They see other women being cherished and showered with attention and affection. They see these women feasting at the table of love that was prepared by the man in their lives. They smell the aroma of love at this banquet prepared just for her and wonder how and why she got stuck with the crumbs of love.

She doesn't realize or even believe she deserves a feast like the other women she sees and may covet. She has not learned the recipe that seats her at the banquet table of love. But in the next few pages of this book she will find out the secrets to being invited to dine at the table instead of wallowing on the floor.

So how did my story end with the Adonis-like specimen of a man I fell in love with? Did I feast at the table or wallow on the floor? My story continued like this:

I could not resist the crumbs. I wallowed on the floor for another 15 years. I had an affair with him, got pregnant with his child, and continued lying to myself about his ability and willingness to invite me to his table. I fell for the carrot-on-a-stick syndrome where he made promises; I believed them and was disappointed over and over again.

I tried to force, manipulate, and worse. I did everything I could to become the prize, not realizing I was already the prize. I was confused, angry and bitter for years to the point I sabotaged every relationship I had with a man. During our breakups I chose abusive, sociopathic, narcissistic guys to bed and wed. I was literally wallowing in the crumbs, I hit rock bottom more than once. My choices were destructive to me and the two children I birthed; wallowing on the floor in the crumbs I might add.

But I eventually got tired of being under the table, bumping my head and accepting the crumbs of excruciating pain, despair, and depression and defeat. I got up and brushed myself off. I looked in the mirror and said, "Enough!" "No more!" I began wiping the crumbs off my body, shook my hair, and determined to learn how to position myself for an invitation to the table and partake of the feast.

For a long time I even bought and set my own table. That was the alternative many women choose. The problem with that was it got lonely at that big table all alone. The kids eventually want to move out and get their own tables so where does that leave me? All alone. I would much rather share my table with a man that has specifically prepared it for me and invites me to his table.

I was finally ready to be cherished and adored by an attentive man. I wanted to be invited in and have my seat pulled out for me and be served a full course meal topped off with delicious cake (not crumbs). And I did! Once I stopped accepting the crumbs in my dating life and relationships, the invitations began coming in. I no longer accept crumbs and I will show you how to get up and stop accepting crumbs too. You will learn the "no more crumbs" dating mantra. You will be set free from dating and relationship purgatory. Are you ready? Let's get started! Let's eat!

I am a 40-year-old, single mother of a teenager who is twice divorced with an MBA and a successful business. I hope the following helps with your book. With an MBA degree, one would think I am pretty smart.

Actually, I am only "book" smart but my abilities to judge a person's character are questionable. I recently left a toxic relationship in which I was physically, verbally and emotionally abused. Entering this relationship seemed easy – he was perfect by all accounts: charming, smart, gainfully employed and respected in the community but behind closed doors, a totally different person. The abuse started slowly, by 3 months, it was all verbal and at 6 months, the physical started. I had already been beat down. I started believing that I was the one with the issue and no one would want me. After all, everyone respected this man.

So I stayed. It is not until he made a move to abuse my daughter did the motherly instinct kick in and I was able to leave.

Kind regards,
Karyn Anjali G.

2 ARE THESE REALLY CRUMBS

Someone asked me how can you know if you are accepting crumbs in your life?

For me the answer is pretty simple. How do you feel when you are with the person? Also, how do you feel when you are away from the person? Paying attention to the core question is key. How do you feel?

Everyone has an internal homing device that allows them know when something feels right and when something feels wrong. Of course we can lie to ourselves and say we feel good because we want to feel good so badly. But when we peel away the layers, walls and chains of denial we will really be able to understand how we really feel.

So the first question is how do you feel when you are with the person? Do you feel consistently validated? Cherished? Protected? Loved? Or do you feel consistently rushed?

Frustrated? Off balance and that something is missing? Is this your dream? Is this what you had in mind for your relationship? Does he make you feel safe and provided for? Does he take you around his family and friends? Does he lift you up and make you feel like the most important person in his life? Do you bloom like a flower?

The next question is how do you feel when you are away from him? There could be a combination of feelings; keep in mind, for you as a woman, feeling or intuition is your guide. If you haven't used her in a while, it's time to dust her off and tune in. She will not lie or go wrong if you are really being honest with yourself. So how do you feel when you are away from him? Do you feel energized after being with him, or do you feel drained? Do you feel neglected or do you feel your needs were met? Can you honestly say he has left you in better shape than before your time together? Is it a relief to be alone or with your friends because you know you will not have to walk on eggshells?

You will know you are getting crumbs in your life by the way you feel when you are with your significant other and how you feel when you are away from that person. There will be a contrast or difference that is too hard to miss. Unfortunately, some women have lost touch with their true selves so it's challenging to really know the truth. There may be a nagging feeling deep down inside. There is something you can't quite put your finger on but you know something is not right. This relationship is not the one you fantasized about when you were a little girl.

Another way to look at it is to imagine this person is with

your daughter (real or imagined). Would the way she is being treated by this same person be what you would want for her? Does she glow and grow in this relationship? If you can say "no" to this question and have the urge to protect and drag your daughter away; if you would advise her to get out of the relationship, you know this is not one you should be in.

So how do you know you are in a crummy relationship with a crummy guy? Your feelings will tell you the truth. Your intuition will guide you. Your little girl will show you. The next step for you is to be honest and courageous enough to let the relationship go and choose yourself first.

DEFINITION OF A CRUMB

The dictionary has several definitions of the word crumb. The most notable one is:

1. A very small piece broken from a baked item, such as a cookie, cake, or bread.
2. A small fragment, scrap, or portion

But did you notice the second definition? Yep, that's the definition I'm referencing in this book. It is what too many women have settled for.

To be clear; a crumb is anything that does not feel right to you. A crumb is anything that does not serve you in a healthy way. A crumb is one of a million ways you are being mistreated, neglected, abused, or ignored.

But a crumb seems so small! Of course they are. They represent all the small things that add up over time that come in a trickle or steady stream. They are thrown at you or simply dropped on the floor for you to come behind and pick up.

Crumbs are not served; they are neglected bits of the banquet or feast being served to someone else. Crumbs are second-hand servings from a very full table that is out of your reach. Crumbs are swept up and thrown away if the dog or cat does not pick them up first.

So imagine you come into a room that has a table filled with delicious foods. You see all your favorites and are ready to dive in. The smell alone just makes your mouth water. Have you ever seen the movie *Antwone Fisher*? He always has this dream where he enters into a room and the table is filled with the most delicious meats, side dishes, salads, and breads. He is welcomed with open arms to sit and eat all he wants. He's basically in heaven. Who wouldn't want to go into a room like that and be welcomed by the smiling faces of people telling you to come on in and eat?

Next, imagine you are escorted to a spot at the table, and then told you will have to sit on the floor next to your significant other. You are not allowed to sit at the table because you are not important enough. But you can have all the crumbs you like. You see the dog lying under the table waiting patiently for the crumbs to start falling and wondering why you don't look excited.

The crumbs are not meant to satisfy you or make you happy. They are tokens to patronize you or small acknowledgments to appease you, so you won't disturb the master.

Are you dating for crumbs?

How can I tell I am dating for crumbs with my date or significant other?

Too often women have this nagging feeling they aren't

being treated the way they should be. They sit around and wait for guys to do the right thing. The truth is, too many will not do the right thing, but will do the thing that is most convenient for THEM. For many, they are not setting out to intentionally hurt the ladies in their lives. They do what they are allowed to do. So the question is, are you deciding to live for crumbs instead of cake?

Dating for crumbs means you are willing to lower your standards and self-respect just to be with and/or have the attention of a man. You let him do one or more of the following 10 things:

1. Accept late night calls
2. Accept excuses for tardiness
3. Accept forgotten birthdays and holidays
4. Accept disrespectful language
5. Accept constant sexual innuendo
6. Accept dates at home instead of out and about
7. Accept his temper or rages or extreme sensitivity to everything
8. Accept pressure to have sex when you want intimacy
9. Accept being invisible
10. Accept being the last priority

We will look at these more in details in the next section/chapter. Review the list carefully and see if this behavior is in your relationships.

Dating for crumbs becomes habitual. It could be you have accepted this kind of behavior from family members or friends for so long, it seems natural to accept it from guys you date. The truth is it is unacceptable if you want to live a quality life. Every person deserves better. Every person deserves respect. The only way to get either is to see your worth and respect yourself.

Dating for crumbs does not have to be something you do for the rest of your life. You can change. The purpose of this book is the help you recognize your value, embrace your freedom of choice, and teach you how to attract the right kind of attention and love into your life.

Why do we date for crumbs?

As mentioned before, we have fallen into the habit of accepting crumbs from significant people in our lives. These people could be parents, siblings, co-workers, supervisors or managers, or even friends.

Crumbs are acceptable to people with low self-esteem because they are getting a reward, no matter how small, from the people who matter most to them. Researchers in the field of mental behavior say some people will do whatever it takes to get attention, even if it is negative. Attention means you feel alive. You are not all alone in this world and have a shot at some form of acknowledgement. It is in our DNA to want attention and affection. However, for some people, if it happens to be crumbs, that is good enough.

It is worth looking deeper into this subject but that is not the focus of this book. Because you are reading this book, it means you are not willing to accept anymore crumbs in your life. You want something different because you deserve something better than the toxic relationships you have been tolerating.

Dating for crumbs is not quality of life. You deserve the cake. I'm here to show you how.

Being smart and being smart about relationships unfortunately have nothing to do with each other. In fact, the higher-order thinking part of your brain is actually separate from the part of your brain that deals with relationships. The relationship part of your brain is hard-wired by your family-of-origin to choose certain types of relationships (Lewis, Amini, & Lannon, A General Theory of Love, 2000).

Vondie Lozano, MFT, Ph.D.
Licensed Marriage & Family Therapist
Relationship Expert
http://vondieslovechats.com/my-story

3 SLOWLY FINDING MYSELF

Over the years I found myself accepting more and more crumbs from crummy guys. They threw a little attention my way and I was hooked. This wasn't always the case. When I was younger, I learned valuable lessons about my worth.

It all started in etiquette classes. Yes, I took etiquette classes, LOL! My parents enrolled my siblings and me because they saw the importance of us knowing how to conduct ourselves in public. This training wasn't just about the correct fork and knife, but it was about valuing yourself.

I learned how to be treated by men through this training. The boys in my class were taught how to open doors for the girls and how to pull the chair out for us. They were taught to walk between the girl and the street as an act of protection. I learned how to receive this treatment and was taught that I was worthy of this treatment.

For a long time I did not remember or understand why I had the sense of self-respect and accepted no-nonsense behavior from guys. I was taught how to be treated so anything different annoyed me.

My dad was instrumental in teaching me how to be treated as well. We had long conversations in my teen years about life, boys, and how to be treated. He taught me about male behavior and showed me by his actions what they should do for the women in their lives. My dad was my protector and provider so I accepted no less from men I dated. It was what I owed myself.

But along the way, I lost some of that self-respect. As I got older and found myself without a significant other I became fearful that I would never meet anyone. This fear drove me to do really stupid things. I accepted crummy behavior from guys in the name of being a good person, a good Christian, and eventually a good wife. But it all backfired on me because I was acting out of fear instead of love.

Loving myself became a low priority because I thought that if I loved myself I was being selfish. I thought loving myself would leave no room for anyone else to love me. I was conflicted and the result was disastrous relationships.

I accepted bad behavior, neglect, disrespectfulness, sexual pressure, abuse, and pretty much everything on the list mentioned in the previous pages. I was living in hell and struggling to find a solid place to put my feet and get my bearings.

The first time I let my guard down and began accepting crumbs was with my first lover. He had a good heart like most people have, but was not 100% available and attentive to me. He had great qualities and spoiled me quite a bit, but he was not all mine. He was battling for visitation rights for his children and entangled in that relationship. I refused to see it clearly and accepted his divided attention.

He was persistent in pursuing me in the beginning. He visited when he could and called when he could, but the distance (30-45 miles) seemed too great most times so I pinned away for him. When he did call or visit it was done in grand style so my anxiousness all but disappeared.

He was exciting to me and made me feel like no other man had ever made me feel. I was addicted to him. The more addicted I became, the more crumbs I accepted. My self-respect diminished and I didn't know how to stand up for myself because I was afraid to lose him. I used manipulation and threats to control him instead of expressing my true feelings.

The relationship was always off balance and on edge. We were both horrible at communication so there were many things left unsaid. We talked about surface things and spent our emotions on mind-blowing sex. The deeper things in life and our relationship were left unsaid.

We broke up a number of times because I was not getting my way and he was not willing to commit 100% due to this custody battle. We were both acting out of fear instead of love and trust. Many promises were made to appease me but few were kept. I grew frustrated and bitter that I was giving so much of myself and he seemed to be giving very little. I was accepting crumbs.

During one of our breakups, he married his children's mother. I found out a month later on one of my rebound attempts. I felt betrayed and devastated but it was partly my fault because I accepted crumbs. The rest of the story was told at the beginning of this book, so I won't go into that again.

I tried to move on after my daughter was born. I didn't date for almost three years but dedicated my life to raising my daughter. I started a business because I wanted to be home with her full-time. I wasn't making ends meet and wanted something more so I got a job at the largest company in the city where I lived. I was minding my own business when a co-worker in another department began pursuing me.

He was not my type or anyone I would have normally dated. My intuition was telling me not to get involved, but I was flattered by the attention. We began talking and going out together after work. Ironically, a few months before I started dating him my daughter had asked me if was I going to get a boyfriend. I took it as a sign and went ahead with this relationship. He was living with his parents, which was a red flag, so we did not go to his place. He ended up at my place often and one day we played hooky from work to go to the mall. We didn't make it and nine months later I gave birth to a baby boy.

Five months into my pregnancy I was feeling the hormonal rush and recalling the conversations I had with this guy. I wasn't sure I wanted to keep the baby initially but knew

I could not kill an innocent child. I threw the idea out of my mind and tried to get on with my life. My boyfriend had other ideas though. I learned he was dating other people so I broke up with him. He began harassing me and even stalking me. I told him we would not be together but I expected him to help take care of this child.

He got cited for sexual harassment at work and was about to be fired when he asked me to vouch for him. I refused because of all I learned about him. I was angry, hormonal and ready to kill someone, but I had accepted crumbs because I wanted the attention and to belong to someone. The last time I spoke to him was during my fifth month of pregnancy. My son has never seen him or received support from him.

But the drama in my life did not end. I was driven by fear and desperation most of the time. I was raising two children on my own and was tired- mentally, emotionally, and physically. I relocated to another city where I was working and going to school full-time because I was determined to make a better life for my children and me. I was determined not to live on welfare or to harass anyone for child support. But the emotional toll was on me and I needed relief.

I was back in communication with my daughter's father. He had gotten a divorce and was living in another city for his job. He was about to leave the country for year when he visited and we tried to reconcile. It went horribly wrong and I fell into depression. I was feeling crummy so I sought the attention of another man to feed my need, help me raise my children, and boost my ego. I wanted to prove to him that someone would love me and marry me since he wouldn't.

I got involved with a man from church that was a part of the single's ministry. We had a whirlwind relationship that ended in marriage and was the start of the most hellacious year and half of my life! Being married to this man started out badly. From day one, he was abusive and crummy. He accused me of everything under the sun. He tried to make me out to be a horrible mother and person. He abused my children and me both mentally, emotionally, spiritually, financially, and sexually. I came to my senses and filed for divorce six months later and within a year we were divorced. This was not before restraining orders, an escape to a battered women's shelter, constant harassment and threats all while finishing school. Talk about crumbs!!!

You would think I would have learned my lessons and been gun shy, but about four years later I began dating an old high school acquaintance. He seemed charming and seemed to have his act together. I learned later it really was just an act. I thought I knew him because of our history so I didn't take the time to really look at the red flags or get to know him. He helped me paint the new house I was buying, and he helped me with a few other things, so he became something of a hero to me. We spent a lot of time together and grew fond of each other. He helped me move into my new house and he moved in as well since he was there so much. We decided to get married because everything seemed so perfect.

He had never been married and didn't have kids but seemed to grow attached to my son. He also helped me get the kids in a private school where a friend of his taught. He influenced a lot of my decisions and charmed me into doing a lot of things I now see was a mistake. He loved to travel so we went on several trips. He also liked to spend money so soon my new credit cards were being used a lot. The only problem was he didn't have a solid job and liked to talk on the phone all day instead of working consistently. The result was he was living off me as he barely brought in enough to pay the mortgage. As the pressure rose, I grew agitated and frustrated with having to do everything on top of dealing with his narcissistic behavior. He thought the world revolved around him so he didn't care how other people felt.

In one of our arguments, he admitted he only wanted to be with me because I could financially support him. Through the months we had been together I could not understand how he could simply not work hard to support this family. I could not understand how it was so easy for him to let me pay for everything and go into debt. From his car to his phone to the roof over his head, I financed. He gloated over it and suddenly it all became clear that he was only with me to use me. He used manipulation and mind games to control me. He even went so far as to withhold sex to control me, which I thought was very immature and suspect.

In many ways I felt like I was reliving my first marriage except there was no constant physical or sexual abuse. On one occasion he did injure me during a disagreement where my chest bone, the sternum, may have been fractured after he put his full weight on me. But I didn't seek medical attention or report it. It was all about verbal, mental and emotional abuse. I hadn't completely healed from my first marriage so I was experiencing PTSD which played out in the current marriage.

Each week I was met with threats of desertion and divorce if we had a disagreement. After a while I began to agree with him and asked for a divorce. I was being verbally abused, threatened with abandonment, supporting him and my children while working and completing a Master's degree program, and trying to start a business too!

When I called his bluff and requested a separation he wanted to know if we could start dating other people. I said the point of the separation was to get counseling and see if we could salvage something. He did not want to do that, but was not willing to get a real job or stop neglecting and treating me badly. He said if we separated that meant we would need to just get a divorce. I agreed and he, though shocked, began living downstairs then eventually moved out. There was more harassment, threats of extreme legal actions, and phone calls to the police.

The divorce papers were served and granted by default. I repossessed the car I financed and was still responsible for paying and let it go to auction. The phone was cut off and I moved on. I did grieve as best I could. I moved away and started life over again with my children. It was important for me to completely heal from all the bad relationships. Eventually, I filed for bankruptcy to get rid of all the debt incurred from that marriage. My house went into foreclosure as well. In a sense, I was given a clean slate and a new life. I got past the shame and guilt I felt and began the process of understanding and loving myself.

I didn't make all the right choices even through the

process. I dated other men and had more crummy experiences but each taught me valuable lessons that would make me really sit up and take notice of my choices in men. In each I sought validation and attention, but each failed miserably because it was simply too much pressure to put on them. I had to find validation in myself and learn what it meant to truly love myself. In loving myself I would no longer be willing to accept crumbs because I knew I deserved the cake!

I lost my father when I was younger and have become very masculine throughout my career as a criminal defense lawyer. I seem to attract men who are emotionally unavailable, married or have a girlfriend. The story I have made up is that men you love leave you or that you are not good enough for the good ones. I have spent most of my adult life attracting the wrong males and have spent the last 10 years alone as a result of not wanting to get hurt any longer. It seems easier to stay away than to get hurt time and time again.

Andrea

---

4 DUSTING OFF THE CRUMBS

After I went through a succession of bad relationship choices I sat down and had a long talk with myself. I was not clear on what I really wanted and what mattered most to me. With much prayer and meditation, I began searching for the meaning of my life and for wholeness.

I learned through reading, prayer, and meditation that what I wanted was what every woman wants. Love. But how could I get or experience this love I so desperately wanted? Why was it so illusive? I had even written a poem on this very topic years earlier. The poem was the questions I asked about love and all about my confusion in this area of my life. Why could I not find love? Why was it always just beyond my reach. In fact here is the poem in it's entirety:

Illusive Love

This aching soul waiting for
Illusive Love
Drowning in despair
Ever wonder when, where
Will love appear?
Through the motions of
Searching deep within
My battered being
To find the key
The reason for this
Illusive Love
Black as the night
Not glimpse of
Love, the future
Seems to hold no
Arms to surround
Me with warmth
So tender, so true
This ever
Illusive Love

I was a seeker of knowledge, wisdom, and love. Where was love? What path should I take to find it? It didn't take long for me to understand and remember that love was right there all the time. It was in my heart and ultimately with God. I heard over and over through the years that God is love and the source of all love.

But I didn't fully understand it, mostly because love was always explained in abstract terms. It was always "out there" somewhere and not readily available to me. Ironically, I had been exercising love each and every day with my children. They changed my life and gave me a reason to live and create a better life for us when things were really hard and depression threatened to suck me under.

I started reading and seeking more of God's love and comparing it to the love a parent has for a child. I compared it to the love I have for my children and had several ah-ha moments! Love wasn't so far away after all. I finally got it and the fog was finally clearing. Love wasn't so elusive. Once I reframed it, learned more about it, and embraced the experiences I was already having, it became easier to see how love would be more prominent in my life.

Discovering self-love

Growing up in a strict religious home and living by rules that threatened to choke the life out of me, I learned that self love was just another term for selfishness. It was steeped in sin and I should have done everything possible to avoid it. I bought it all- hook, line, and sinker. No wonder I had such low self-worth and low self-esteem. Anytime I tried to climb out of the barrel, I was pulled back in through guilt, shame, and criticism.

But I was tired of living that way. I had to discover who I was and live my own life. I had to start becoming the best me possible. But how was that possible if I didn't even like who I was and was ashamed of myself?

My relationships were a glaring clue that something was wrong and missing in my life. How could a reasonably intelligent, talented, and successful woman do so poorly in relationships? How could I be such a failure in a sea of so much information? I found myself swimming in a sea of crumbs and still felt just as lonely and dissatisfied as before.

I didn't know how to stop losing myself in relationships. I didn't know how to stop giving so much and depleting my emotional and financial resources. I was tired of giving and giving and never receiving. This was not my ideal life and it was not working for me.

In my typical fashion, I began searching for answers. I went online and typed in the word, "self love" or something similar. I came across a few articles and a book I eventually bought titled, *Choosing Me Before We: Every Woman's Guide to Life and Love*. I read excerpts on Google Books and decided to buy it.

I read the first few chapters, and my life was changed. It was such an eye opener for me. All my life I put others ahead of me. It is partly because of my up-bringing and partly because of religion. I was living the life everyone else wanted me to live. I was living to make everyone else comfortable and not rock the boat. I was living and dying at the same time.

I learned through this book and other articles that I have to put myself first before any relationship. This does not make me selfish but gives me more energy to love and be there for others. It makes my relationships healthier. We have all heard the advice flight attendants give at the beginning of a flight. They tell us to give ourselves oxygen before helping others in the case of an airline emergency. It was finally clicking that I can't be effective or more loving if I am trying to love on empty.

If my love tank is completely depleted I have nothing to give. I have to give from my overflow in order to be my best me and give of myself. And this does not mean giving the best of myself. I have to give myself the best I have to offer so others benefit from the rich residuals of my life.

What is real love?

The concept of love became even clearer after watching a documentary one day called, "Love," by Dr. Gary Null. I was so blown away by the concepts discussed in the film. In essence, love is energy that expands and changes everything when we learn how to embrace it. We are all energy and when we allow love to enter in and become a part of our lives we are able to do more, give more, and be more in the world.

The experts in this film took it a step further and expanded on love. The featured experts all agreed that love is God. Love is a spiritual experience. What we call love is often neediness. The love songs on the radio, the people crooning in misery, are not really love. It is all emotional wounds projected out into the world.

True love is energy that revitalizes the soul and makes the person open to it feel light and joyful. It is not easily broken but is the stuff solid foundations are made of. True love is strong and affirming. The stuff of I Corinthians 13 in the Bible comes to life when real love is present.

I used to think it was hard to be patient, kind, long suffering and basically humble. But when I understood the true meaning of love it became easy. How? These characteristics are a natural result of love's energy. When your life is rooted in love the rest is easy.

Not only are the traits of love easy to live out for others, it becomes easier to express for yourself. Self-love becomes easier to grasp and live each day. When I got it, I was able to be patient, kind, long suffering, and humble with myself. When I was able to do that, I could offer it to others.

Putting it into practice

Now that I understand that self-love is possible and good, my life has changed. I see relationships differently. My intentions have changed. Life has become a continuous succession of joy. I wake up each day with a determination to have a great day. This affects every decision I make. It affects my relationships. I no longer fall into depression that lasts for days and weeks. My hormones have stabilized and I am just happier.

The world sees the results through my smile and generosity. This makes me more attractive to quality men. I am now attracting really great people and relationships. I have a fuller life and so much joy. All this is possible because I now practice self love. It is the foundation of a No More Crumbs life.

Each morning I wake up and meditate as well as offer praise and gratitude for my life and all the incredible gifts I receive each day. I think about love and how I want it to fill me up and expand my world. I ask for love from the source of love and He is faithful to give it to me. I can never ask for too much because there is an endless supply for me and everyone who wants it.

In the shower, I think about how great life is. Sometimes I dance a little jig, without slipping and falling of course, and I lift my arms to the sky and request love to be poured into my heart. The shower water beating on my chest is symbolic of love being poured into my heart. It is a simple act but very profound to me! More importantly it works!

Your Story?

So what is your story? How have you been accepting and settling for crumbs in your relationships? Is it working for you? Too often we settle because we think we can't do any better or we feel obligated to stay with this person because they supply us with basic needs. They "let" us into their lives and keep us around. But the emptiness in the pit of your stomach, that hole in your heart is a sign you deserve better.

Keep in mind that this is true for women who are in relatively good mental health. If you are suffering from bipolar disorder, schizophrenia, or any other mind altering illness please get the help you need. This book is not for you.

Your story, your reason for picking up this book has to be because you know you deserve better relationships. It's not just about dating, but about every relationship you have. Waiting by the table and waiting for a few crumbs of attention, protection, and affection is beneath you.

It's time for a wake up call; a jolt that will shake you out of your mental fog. Aren't you tired of waiting by the phone wondering if he is going to call? Aren't you fed up with not being heard? Aren't you over being taken for granted? What does it take to help you see your value? How many times do you have to be ignored to understand your worth?

In the next few pages I will teach you how to recognize your worth, embrace your freedom, and attract the love you deserve. When you have finished reading this book you will know just how important you are in this world. You will understand the importance of putting yourself first. You will learn how to shine so brightly with love that you attract the right kind of man and relationships that make you shine even brighter!

You will feel more love.
You will raise your self-esteem.
You will find soulful work.
You will position yourself for your soul mate.

So get your pen and highlighter out to take notes and mark this book up. You will want to remember all the important points. You will probably make a few people angry and you may lose a few friends, but this only means you are making room for new friends and better relationships.

So let's get to work. Your future is waiting!

I met someone when I was 17 at a college university gathering. We became friends during the year and I respected his values: he was kind, polite, patient, and very important to me, spiritual. I did not take dating casually, being raised in a South Indian household, and when we made the decision to begin 'courting' it was with the express purpose (he said) to pursue marriage. This was music to my ears because I did want to be a wife and had been raised to expect this as a sign of arriving to adulthood.

As our relationship continued, there were promises he extracted from me in exchange for being the kind of guy who could "handle me" or put up with my liberal views (which we both agreed many others in our conservative community would not). This in addition to the fact that he didn't mind my being brown, actually learned to find it attractive, convinced me that I couldn't break the promise I had made to love this person. So I did. For six years, through several moves (me always) to different states, finishing one degree, then another graduate one, into yet a third. I didn't write for our university paper because it would upset him; I suffered through going to events alone on nights he was busy or didn't feel up to being around people. I essentially lived a double life, one without him where I was developing academically and another where I was the patient, kind woman behind her man.

Eventually, I moved to another country and the first morning there I woke up and thought: "What have I been doing?" Needless too say, that was the last time we spoke, and I never saw him again, though he persisted for another six months in insisting that he loved me. If that was love, I wanted no part of it.

Mohana

Section II

5 LEARNING THE WRONG MESSAGE

How many times have your attempted to do something daring and bold and been shut down by the voices in your head? It's pretty frustrating to always give into fear isn't it? But that is what we do each day. We decide today is the day I'm going to leave him and find a better relationship.

We say the same thing about out jobs, our toxic families, and our frenemies. But we put it off just one more day because today they are saying all the right things and doing the things you love. But tomorrow is right around the corner with all its misery. The crazy thing is you are right there again wishing you could fly off to an exotic (and exclusive) location to escape it all.

So why do we listen to the voices in our heads? What purpose do they serve? In the beginning, they were there to keep us safe and direct our paths. Children need those voices to remind them not to cross the street in oncoming traffic. Teens need those voices to keep them from getting stoned out of their minds the night before final exams. But as an adult, you've learned all the lessons and know all the methods for staying out of harm's way. So why do we keep the voices? The voices once represented safety and security, but in adulthood they take on a stalker-like persona and will not leave you alone! Every move you make comes under the scrutiny of the voice. You begin to look over your shoulder all the time, afraid to make a wrong move.

So who are these voices? Where did they come from? Voices represent authority figures from parents, teachers, public officials, and a number of other people you see as credible and reliable sources of information. They are the ones who were helpful when you were a child but are a hindrance now that you are an adult. They served their purpose and now it's time to fire them, release them, or let them go harass someone else.

They are the ones who tell you that loving yourself is selfish. They nag you about wearing your clothes too tight or wearing too much makeup. They make you feel guilty every time you eat a piece of double fudge brownies. They tell you it is unreasonable to quit your job and move to your dream location to start over. The voices keep you stuck and in a cycle of pain. They keep you safe and walled in so you never experience true joy. They keep you from knowing who you really are and discovering what makes you unique, loveable, and worthy of a non-toxic relationship.

So your first order of business is to ditch the criticism committee, the voices, and the naysayers. It may feel like murder in the first degree but it is for your own good and for your happiness. Remember at the end of the day you have to live with every decision you make.

Diving In Head First

Now that you have dumped the voices, it's time to examine your relationships head on. What's working for you and what's not working for you? Is it worth keeping this relationship? Is there something you can salvage (but really, who wants a salvaged item when you can get a shiny new item)?

Why do you choose crummy men? What is the point? Do they start out crummy? That is a key question. Sometimes we meet men who are probably good people. They are nice enough and may treat us well in the beginning, but something happens to change all of that. We are going to take a look under the hood to get to the bottom of this to find out why it changed.

You cannot blame the guy for everything. Some of it must fall on your lap missy! We are responsible for our own outcomes. Every action we take; every decision we make is the result of an earlier choice. This chain of events brought you to this point. But don't worry, we will figure it all out and turn you on to a better way of living and loving.

So you have a guy who started out hot and heavy for you. He showered you with attention and affection. You were the star in his crown and the apple of his eye. You were seated across from him at the table of love eating moist, scrumptious cake. You gazed into each other's eyes and giggled like school kids. He couldn't get enough of you and you were on cloud nine. Literally, floating when you walked.

But something happened and now you find yourself under the table with the dog waiting for a few crumbs to fall. You feel neglected and unattractive. You struggle to get him to look you in the eyes. He has all kinds of excuses for why he doesn't have time for you, won't provide for you, and won't protect you. He may not say the words but his actions are loud and clear.

You feel needy and clingy and desperate for some kind of attention or touch. But it's few and far between. When he needs you to do something for him, he briefly turns his attention back on you. He throws you a few crumbs and the day is saved. He's your hero again until the next day, week or month.

You are on a rollercoaster ride and always feel off balance. You can't put your finger on it but you know something is not right. Your conversations are laced with his self-defensiveness. He is ultra sensitive and moody. He doesn't call, email, or even text. It feels like days and weeks go by before you have a conversation. He doesn't return your calls within minutes anymore; it takes hours or days. He assures you that he loves you, but you are not feeling the love. It is painful to think he might have found someone else but that couldn't be the reality. Or could it?

The painful truth is if you want a different tomorrow you must begin facing reality today. You must tell the truth and be honest with yourself about your circumstances. It is time to take a deeper look at the crumbs you are living for. It is time to put a magnifying glass up to the situation you are accepting in your life and begin asking questions that will get to the heart of the matter. This is for you. It is for your future. So let's dive in and see how you got lost in a sea of crumbs.

My second husband was physically abusive. To the world, we had a great marriage and family of blended children. He would hit me in my torso so no marks would show. I did not come from an abusive home as a child but he did. My abusive ex husband was a textbook in describing domestic violence and how he wooed me and then alienated me from both my family and friends. I got out slowly through one important document at a time. I was not afraid at the time in my lack of knowledge but it was very dangerous. I tell women all the time that involving friends and family places them at risk too. I escaped on my own and got back on my feet on my own.

D.B.
Bold Selah, LLC
www.Boldlioness.com

Samantha A. Gregory

6 LOST IN A SEA OF CRUMBS

In an earlier chapter I talked about how to recognize you are living for crumbs. I promised we would examine each one of the signs. This is your magnifying glass looking at the situation, so prepare to become uncomfortable. No one likes to hear about his or her issues and mess. But it is necessary if you want to move into a better way of living and attract the kind of love you've always wanted.

Many of us have been lost in a sea of crumbs for years. It became a way of life and for many, quite a comfortable life. But something just wasn't right. What happened to the fairy tale life you dreamed about?

Have you given in to "reality" and decided to wake up or give up?

What about living happily ever after with the man of your dreams? Is that no longer possible or an option for you?

Is it because you've invested so much time, money, energy, and effort into the relationship?

Is it because of the kids?

Is it because you are afraid of what other people may think?

No matter what the reason you owe it to yourself to open your eyes and see how deep the issues run.

I find there are 10 major ways we get lost in a sea of crumbs. They are all the situations and treatments you accept from the guys you date and mate. This list is not exhaustive, but it represents the most common things you allow. We will look at them in detail. In the second part of this book, we will discover how to turn the crumbs into cake because you deserve it! You'll see. So let's see this list.

10 Crumbs Women Accept

1. Accepting late night calls
2. Accepting excuses for tardiness
3. Accepting forgotten birthdays and holidays
4. Accepting disrespectful language
5. Accepting constant sexual innuendo
6. Accepting dates at home instead of out and about
7. Accepting his temper, rages, or extreme sensitivity to everything
8. Accepting pressure to have sex when you really want intimacy
9. Accepting being invisible
10. Accepting being the last on the list of his priorities

This list goes from the simple to the complex. It is meant to help you think about the different types of crumbs you have been accepting. Some seem innocent enough but they have a deeper underlying meaning or assumption being made on his part and perhaps yours. They are all rooted in one fatal flaw in the relationship. Your lack of self-respect and self-love. Don't get upset with me now. You probably thought it was all about him and what he isn't doing. But sweetheart it's all about you too and what you are accepting and allowing. Those words are interchangeable.

To accept means to allow, so the list could have easily read:

1. Allowing late night calls
2. Allowing excuses for tardiness
3. Allowing forgotten birthdays and holidays
4. Allowing disrespectful language
5. Allowing constant sexual innuendo
6. Allowing dates at home instead of out and about
7. Allowing his temper or rages or extreme sensitivity to everything
8. Allowing pressure to have sex when you want intimacy
9. Allowing being invisible
10. Allowing yourself to be last on his list of priorities

So, you see there is really no difference in the meaning or with whom the responsibility lays. It belongs to you. The good thing about owning responsibility is you also have the power to change the situation.

Let me make it very clear to you again. YOU HAVE THE POWER! You have always had the power, but you have believed you didn't have any or you simply relinquished it to gain, what you thought was going to be, love from a man.

But it's okay. You probably didn't know or remember that

you have the power to change your life and relationships. But I'm here to remind you and show you how to turn the negative things you've accepted and allowed into a positive experience that brings the relationship you want and deserve.

Now let's examine these crumbs. They are getting a little too messy and a whisk broom will not sweep them all up. We are going to need a vacuum.

7 STUPID THINGS WOMEN ACCEPT IN DATING/RELATIONSHIPS

Accepting/Allowing Late Night Calls

This is for the ladies who are dating and/or have a boyfriend. This is for teen and college girls who want to start things off right because the truth is, how you begin the relationship sets the tone for the rest of it.

Accepting or allowing late night calls seems innocent enough. You like this guy a lot and want to spend as much time as possible talking to him. He says he likes you and wants to get to know you. It all sounds good and you are just excited that any guy is calling you. But this is not the best way to start a relationship.

Imagine a young lady has caught the attention of a very cute guy. They have a class together and all the other girls think he is quite a catch. Every day they wonder whom he will smile at during 5th period. They are all giggles when he walks into the room. Then one day he notices you. He smiles and finds a way to sit by you. He strikes up a conversation and pretty soon you are all smiles and blushing. He finally asks for your number because he wants to compare class notes. You scribble it down in a hurry or enter it into his cell phone, heart pounding because he is going to call. You wait in anticipation and check your phone every three minutes wondering if it's him. You get irritated when it's one of your friends calling or texting because you want to keep the line free. Finally, he calls. It's 11:30 at night and you are half asleep. His voice sounds so sexy and you force yourself to wake up to chat with him. He doesn't mention the notes from class but says he wants to get to know you. You almost melt with glee and chat way into the night.

This scenario could easily be a guy at the office, at your church, or at the gym. It doesn't matter because it plays out just the same. He promises to call, you get excited, you wait, and he calls at an ungodly hour. So what's wrong with that you ask? What's wrong is you set the stage for him to think he can call you anytime he wants and you will answer. Now let's look at the same scenario. It has been a few months since the first late night call.

You and Mr. Hotness are an item now. You are getting to know each other and you go on dates at least three times a week. Since you have been dating your grades are slipping and you are always tired. What you don't know is he goes home to take a nap each afternoon and gets up late (and refreshed) to start socializing.

You are diligent in studying after school, you have a job, and you like spending time with your friends and family. By the end of the day you are dog-tired and need sleep. Your new guy calls when it's convenient for him and takes up the time that could be spend sleeping.

You say you don't mind but deep down it irritates you that he calls so late. You brought it up a couple of times but he makes excuses or brushes you off telling you that you didn't mind a couple of months ago. By now you are afraid he might start calling someone else so you suck it up just to keep him happy and because you don't want to lose him.

So the innocent late night phone calls turns into an internal struggle to get your voice heard and your needs met. You are taken for granted and disrespected. But it didn't have to be this way. Had you been aware of how things could have turned out, the choice may have been different. You may have said something different as you handed over your number. You may have asked a couple of more questions during your initial conversation.

Now you are feeling stuck and are getting tired of being tired every doggone day! So what is the price of accepting and allowing late night calls? Being taken for granted and feeling disrespected. It leaves you feel quite crummy...

Allowing excuses for tardiness

You and your guy have been dating for a while but he has a bad habit of being late. We are not talking a few minutes late; we are talking hours late. There are a variety of reasons why he is habitually late and some of the reasons why may be legitimate, but are enough of an excuse to keep you waiting. He thinks you are obligated to wait for him and expects you to behave as if nothing happened. He probably gets offended and defensive if you bring it up or is upset when he finally arrives.

The trouble is you have allowed this behavior to continue. The first and second time you allowed him to keep you waiting set the stage for each incident. Maybe you thought it was okay at first. Maybe you made excuses for him, telling yourself he just can't be on time. Maybe you were so happy to be going out at all, you told yourself it didn't matter. Now here you are, waiting for him to arrive. His lateness has caused you to miss movies, reservations, and other important events like weddings, and your nephew's bar mitzvah. It's getting pretty serious here lady.

This kind of behavior is another manifestation of crumminess in your life.

Allowing forgotten birthdays and holidays

This is a big one but one that happens quite often in crummy relationships. Your birthday is in a week and you've been dropping hints about what you want. You've even asked about the plans for the night like what should you wear, do you need a sweater, etc.

The day and night goes on and you either wait for him to show up and surprise you or you sit at your place waiting for a phone call. But nothing happens. No phone call, no email, no pick-up. Just crickets and tears filling your eyes. You wonder what happened and go to bed in despair. Your friends and family call and send you cards and gifts but your guy doesn't do anything for you. His excuse is he forgot.

But he not only forgets your birthday, he forgets Valentine's Day and Christmas too. His excuse is he does not celebrate or buy gifts during holidays because they have become so commercialized. He does all this, despite the fact he accepts your gifts and would be angry if you forgot or ignored his birthday.

I have a history of toxic relationships in my past and I have had to take a very hard look at the pattern of toxic men in my life and the root of my involvement with them. With the help of supportive friends and counselors, I realized that my poor self-esteem and loneliness led me to settle for men that were disrespectful, dishonest and downright abusive.

I was "in love with being in love" and got an adrenaline rush in the early stages of dating a man, when everything seemed wonderful and I was showered with attention, compliments and affection. As time went on, however, my partner's behavior would change and abuse began creeping into the relationship in subtle ways. Before I knew it, I was in a full-blown toxic relationship and in the same-old-same-old cycle.

I have learned to set strong boundaries and to enforce them and to spot warning signals right away. I have not been in a dating relationship for 10 years and though singleness may not be for everyone, I have never felt more secure and more confident than I do now because I have no one chipping away at my self-worth, trying to convince me that I'm crazy, or abusing me. I have learned to stop looking to others to meet my needs by turning to God, who is father to the fatherless and defender of widows.

T. O.

Allowing disrespectful language

In the last few years it seems it has become acceptable for the mainstream and the general public to use profanity in every conversation. The movies are filled with these words as well as commercial television. It seems you can't escape it. Some say it's just a normal part of life and everybody is doing it. You may even be doing it, so if you are not bothered by your guy's language and don't find it disrespectful, feel free to move on to the next section. For those who cringe every time a dirty word comes out of his mouth, read on.

Allowing profanity and other disrespectful language is accepting crumbs. The guy has a right to know how you feel about it. He has a right to a couple of warnings, but it should not be a battle you have to fight each time you talk. You should not have to be assaulted in every private conversation you have with him. If your ears are burning or you feel dirty with every conversation, you owe it to yourself to speak up or stop speaking to him altogether.

I don't think I have to spell out the words to shun because we all know them or have heard them at least once in our lives.

If your guy insists on using disrespectful language because he says he can't help it or simply he can say whatever he wants, then you have a choice to keep him and listen to it or let him go. What it does to you is demean you bring you down to a common level in his eyes. If he is not willing to refrain in your presence, he is not willing to do other important things for you. He does not cherish you and does not respect you. That's pretty crummy.

Allowing constant sexual innuendo

Like bad language, it has become the norm for men to use sexual innuendo with the women they date. For some reason they think this is cute and laugh it off. You are on the receiving end, so it is not funny. Some of you may like it and think I should lighten up, but I simply cannot and will not lighten up.

Allowing this constant barrage of suggestive language with a guy you are not even married to is to demean and disrespect yourself. It's only harmless play you might say or be thinking. Actually, it is a test to see how willing you are for sex with him.

If you accept this kind of behavior you are sending a signal that he reads as you are willing to go to bed with him. You are saying you don't mind him talking about your body parts or referring to sexual situations or positions. You don't mind him being crude and referring to his body parts or sexual activities. As with accepting bad language, accepting this kind of behavior sets you up to being disrespected and being no better than a prostitute.

Granted, men are visual and they notice when you have a nice body or a particularly spectacular body part. They think about sex a lot too. But for a guy to constantly talk about it to the exclusion of everything else, you've got a crummy guy on your hands. You will probably find yourself in a compromising position before you know it. If you have been in a relationship for a while, that started out with you allowing sexual innuendo and/or had sex early in the relationship, you probably find yourself with a gaping hole in your soul and a lot of dissatisfaction. That is why you picked up this book. You want something more. You want the cake.

Allowing dates at home instead of out and about

When you first meet a guy who says he likes you, he makes a date with you. You go out to dinner and a movie or some other outing. But pretty soon he starts hinting at wanting to taste some of your cooking. He might say he's running low on funds but still wants to see you so you invite him to your place or you go to his. The next thing you know, one of those two places is where you end up all the time.

You settle into a routine and rarely if ever, go out anymore. You watch TV or a movie, order in or you cook something. When you ask about going out he wants to know why because you all seem to be having a great time staying in. You are like a little married couple.

Soon he starts going out with the guys or hanging out with coworkers after work and leaving you at home (or his place because you have a key now) to get along without him. He only hangs around when he's hungry or wants something from you. Now you are caught in a difficult situation. You are being taken for granted and disregarded because you have allowed home dates too soon or too often. You are starting to feel crummy and stuck because you want his attention and affection.

Allowing his temper or rages or extreme sensitivity to everything

Your guy has a temper. He is set off by the smallest things but you think it's cute at first. He defends you against other guys and you feel safe and wanted. But pretty soon he turns his temper on you. At first he shouts but quickly apologizes and makes the excuse he's had a bad day. You let it go, but it happens again over something trivial. How could you leave the car door unlocked the whole time we were in the restaurant? You idiot!

Your feelings are hurt but you feel better because he apologizes and brings you flowers. The problem is this pattern continues over the next few months. His temper flares more frequently and you sit still until it passes. His boss, his job, his family are all idiots and deserve his wrath.

Your guy may not be that extreme. He may just be sensitive to playful joking or you laughing at a blunder he made. He sulks and rejects you until you apologize 15 times. He accuses you of disrespecting him anytime you stand up and defend yourself when he hurts your feelings. If you spend time talking to your family and friends on the phone a little too long, he is offended. If you buy the wrong color tie on his birthday, he is offended. If you say the "wrong" thing or don't read his mind or intentions just right, you have something against him. This is a lot of pressure and is a very stressful way to live; yet many of you are living this way right now. You can get off the roller coaster and find your way to freedom. Keep reading. I'll show you how.

Allowing pressure to have sex when you want intimacy

In our sex crazed world, it seems everywhere you turn there is somebody having sex. The reality is most couples aren't having that much sex because they are too busy working and/or raising kids. What we see on television and in the movies is often over the top and misleading. But too many men would have you thinking everybody is doing it, so they pressure you into having sex when all you really want is intimacy.

It becomes a battle of wits to see who will win. But why should it be a battle for anything? Unfortunately, women give in to having sex too early or too often because they think it is the only way to get intimacy. But men who do not love you or have an emotional attachment to you do not feel or get intimacy from sex. They just get a physical release and you are left feeling empty.

Intimacy is a heart to heart exchange that does not come from premature sex. When intimacy is achieved then sex becomes more meaningful. Before then, it is mostly just an act of self-gratification for the guy.

He may promise you everything under the sun to get you to cave in to the pressure. Nice dinners, the right words, and massages are all tools he uses to make the sex act happen quickly and frequently. This is how he is built. You still have to make the final choice though, but he's found out all the things you like and will use them to get what he wants.

This does not make him a bad person, but it is bad for you if you succumb to his advances before you get what you need first. You will be unfulfilled in the act each time you don't get the intimacy you really want. You may say it doesn't matter or you don't have to have it, but you really need it. It's all a part of the cake and having the relationship you dreamed of and deserve.

Allowing him to make you the invisible woman

This is sometimes quite hard to pinpoint in the early stages of the relationship. But it becomes quite apparent in later stages. You can't help but feel the vague sense of being invisible to him. Your actions and activities go unnoticed. It starts with long hours at work or out with the guys. It includes long periods of silence on the ride to church or other events. When you speak there is only a grunt or no response at all. When his family or friends are in the room you are completely ignored.

Conversations go over your head or around your body. You are good enough to serve lemonade or coffee to everyone but not regarded otherwise. It could be days before he asks you a direct question or acknowledges your presence. His excuse is he is preoccupied with work or some other problem. You find yourself out on your own taking classes, going to movies, or being with friends.

The only time he pays any attention to you is when he wants/needs sex. He may speak to you in the morning on the way to work and then he is asking if you feel like having sex tonight. You sigh and say you guess so. "Good!" he says and walks out with a spring in his step.

Even in lovemaking you feel invisible. The lights are off and he gropes around until he finds you. He fondles you a bit to "arouse" you and then enters you, pumps a few times and is done. He does not call your name, linger over your favorite areas, or caress you. It's all mechanical. Or he takes you and makes love to you but it feels like he's thinking of someone else the entire time.

He doesn't notice your new outfit, your new haircut, or your new anything. You live separate lives and orbit around a child, a home, or a business. There is clearly no intimacy and it feels like there is no "you." How crummy is that?

Allowing yourself to become last on his list of priorities

How many times have you fallen in line behind work, parents, siblings, friends, kids, dogs and God knows how many other people and events? It seems you are never a top priority. Whenever you want time alone or attention you get pushed aside. You have to wait until everyone else's needs are met before you are even considered. He says it's because he's important or he's a nice guy and cannot help being there for others. He says you should be grateful to have such a generous guy for a boyfriend/husband. All you feel at this point is resentful.

You are tired of being on the back burner, and you want more. But you feel selfish (or the seed has been planted in your head by someone) for wanting more of his time. He is doing such good work in the community. In order to get time with him you have to be in the trenches with him but that's not your personality or interest, and frankly it's all too tiring. It would be okay for him to be involved a couple of days out of the week, but it is constant, seven days a week of activities. This is the good guy scenario.

But your guy may have no interest in being a good guy. He may be the one who is constantly working because he wants to get ahead or keep up with the Joneses. Every waking moment is spent trying to get more and prove his worth. But in the process, he puts you and your needs last. He says you should be happy to have all the nice things he buys you but the truth is, it hurts to be ignored and taken for granted. In fact it's kind of crummy.

The stages of these behaviors have progressed from meeting a new guy to living with him to being married or in a long-term relationship with him. You can see how each stage moves into a deeper level of crumminess. I explained each to give you a sense of the signs and symptoms of crummy relationships. You probably saw yourself in many of the scenarios. It doesn't feel good knowing you have allowed these behaviors over the last few weeks, months, or years. But there is hope and no need to beat yourself up over it. There is a way to change all this and begin having the cake you deserve. We will dive into a new way of thinking, changing, and behaving so you get all you dreamed of having in this relationship or a new one.

I was 16 when I met this boy, and he was 17. He had gotten out of jail and from the beginning, the relationship was doomed to fail. He had no sense of respect but at that age I was attracted to the "bad boy." How bad he actually was, I would soon find out!

He would argue with me and belittle me constantly. He even began physically abusing me after the verbal abuse. He raped me as well and would be continuously disrespectful and deeming. He stole money from me. I became pregnant and aborted the child because he was just out of control and was of no support to me.

It finally clicked in my head when I was 21 and had been broken up with him for a few years, that I thought I was searching for love. I have a very loving set of parents who are both in my life and had always been a great support to me. I was rebelling, I think, because they were strict. I think that the reason that most women stay in toxic relationships is because that they are too far gone. They get mentally abused to the point that they cannot gain their self-esteem back. It takes a lot of time and the scars last for a while.

I am 25 now and am finally confident in my own skin and in a healthy relationship.

Alli

8 HOW TO CHANGE THE STORY

Now you see how toxic relationships work. You hopefully understand what it means to accept crumbs in a relationship. So now what? What do you do with this information? You could forget about it and go on with your life because you accept your lot in life.

Things are not perfect but you can live with the crumbs because you at least have a man. You could be very content with having someone to call your own and sleep with each night. The financial tradeoff outweighs any need for happiness and is too costly to make way for your dreams.

If that is your story or your thought process, you can choose to stay in the same story. That is certainly your right. But if you are tired of wallowing around in the crumbs and want a different life, I urge you to read on.

The Crumbs aren't that Great

Okay so the crumbs aren't that great. You are tired of waiting for a crumb to fall. You simply want more. Living with crumbs has become a bore and a chore. Why continue living this way? What is the point?

We've seen how a relationship looks when you accept behaviors that do not make you feel loved, accepted, and cherished. Deep down inside they hurt your feelings and make you feel worthless. Every woman wants to feel cherished and secure. Some think you can't have both, but I do not agree. You can have both because they really go hand in hand. To feel cherished is to feel secure and you can have that if you are willing to change your behavior.

Yes, I said change your behavior. If you are not changing your behavior or your thought process then nothing will change in your life. You are the person accepting/allowing the crumbs. You are the person reading this book. You are the person who wants a changed life. This process is not as easy as 1-2-3. It takes dedication and commitment to move from your present state of mind and living to a better way of life. You've got to learn the ropes or learn a new recipe and discover how to make your own cake. When you've done that, quality men will be lining up for a chance to sit you at their table instead of bumping you off to the floor where you will only get crumbs.

Learning the Ropes

Changing your behavior is within your power. If you look at human behavior you see people really don't change unless there is an incentive or something that will benefit them in a permanent way. Sure people change (temporarily) to get instant gratification. They change for a few weeks or months to reap a reward, but the change is not lasting. People typically fall back into their same patterns whether they are destructive or not.

The thing that evokes change is the thing that will bring permanent reward and lasting benefit. Becoming conscious of what is not working and/or a painful experience prompts thoughts and necessary action to move past and into a better way of life.

To learn a new way of thinking and behaving you must make a decision. This decision involves going into yourself for a brief time and examining the events that lead up to your current situation. How did it happen? What steps did you take to get here? Most importantly, you must recognize your habits and thoughts because they are powerful.

This exercise is in essence playing the "Who Am I" game. Asking a series of questions and taking a hard look at the answers can be scary and challenging. Do we really want to look at ourselves in the mirror and see our weaknesses? Typically, that is what we look for, but I suggest you look at your strengths more.

What are your best features?

What do you do extremely well?

What do people who admire you say about you?

What are your talents and skills?

How did you get to be such a great person?

This last question may seem like an odd one to ask because you probably don't feel like such a great person. If you were, how did you get to this place? How did you end up in such a bad or toxic situation? But the reality is we are all great in our own way. We contribute something wonderful to the world because we are all unique.

If you have a hard time accepting this, it is no wonder you are so easy to accept crumbs in your life. But it is a process to accept the truth about who you are as a person and as a unique and wonderful contributor of life on this planet. I guarantee that when you get this and accept this, your life will change. You will not be tempted or willing to accept crumbs any longer. You will only reach for and accept the cake you deserve!

Getting a Taste of Cake

By now you are either confused or excited. What is the next step? How do you get a taste of the cake? It goes back to recognizing your value in this world. You have to continue playing the "Who Am I" game. In this section, it is all about discovering your value and worth. When you understand how valuable and worthy you are to have great relationships and a great life, it will be easier to move into the next section of this book where I share the secrets to getting the cake.

But for now I urge you to really study this section and really get it because the next section will not work as effectively if you skip this exercise. You may understand the techniques in your head but if your heart and spirit are not in it, you will resort to accepting crummy behavior again.

You will experience life on the other side of crumbs for a little while, but your behavior will attract more crummy men and you will go around saying this book didn't work. You will be miserable and continuously searching and reading more books to no avail because you tried to skip this section. Even if you do skip on and read about the techniques, at least come back to this section to understand how and why what I'm about to say makes such a big difference in your permanent outcome. Promise me, promise yourself that you will, okay?

Who Am I?

This is the million dollar question, isn't it? This is the question of the ages and of every person who walks this earth at some point. Who am I and why am I here? The answers often allude or hide from us. They seem to be a mystery. We ask this question because from day one we are groomed and shaped to be what others want us to be. The process is either active or passive. Someone is directly or indirectly involved in shaping our lives. They tell us what to think, what to feel, who we are, and give a million and one commands to be, do, act the way they want us to act.

For women it seems especially true. Our mothers dress us up, shut us down, bend, twist and pull us in so many directions. Our fathers notice us, ignore us, shun us, or smother us. Then there are the teachers and preachers and doctors who all have the best intentions and advice to give us. The books, magazines, and television shows we watch infer how we should behave and who we should become.

We have a million messages coming at us at a million miles an hour. We get overwhelmed with trying to be everything to everyone. We bend and contort to the point of breaking. We wear layers of masks and change them to fit the occasion.

They become such a huge part of who we are that we are

afraid to remove them completely because we are afraid the world can't really handle the real self. We become prisoners. Is it no wonder more women are depressed than men? Is it surprising that more women are on antidepressants and other prescription drugs than men?

Are we surprised that more women are overweight, especially in America, than men because food has become the drug of choice? We suppress our anger and rage with food, prescription drugs, and for many, alcohol. We hate ourselves, yet we put on a smile and wear the mask so they won't know about our pain.

These masks and coping mechanisms cripple our hearts, so could that be the reason heart disease is the number two killer in women? The organ that represents the center of woman's essence is damaged and destroyed because it lacks freedom and love. But why? How did this happen? How did we get to this place? How did the gender that colors the world and makes it bright and beautiful come to wear masks and drab shades of grey? How did all the pretty little girls become cynical, bitter, and beat down women who are willing to accept crumbs? This is not what we were created to be.

Many factors played a role in the demise of the feminine woman full of life and who dined only on cake. We have lost our intuition, the precious part of us that guides our lives and gives it meaning. We have lost it and are having a terrible time finding it again. So we must go back to the beginning. We must learn, understand and accept basic truths about who we are as women. The wonderful thing about it is, there is hope and it can be such wonderful new experience for you when you hear all about it.. The crazy thing is, it is so simple you will not believe it.

The issue was never how smart I was. The issue was how I believed I deserved to be treated, and I found several men who were willing to treat me that way.

I learned how I deserved to be treated by men from my dad: speaking sexually about other women in front of me; being kind and loving to everyone but me; and much more. I found men who were cruel in those same ways.

It wasn't until I started healing through the trauma left behind by my dad that my relationships with other men started improving. I began to learn that it was my dad who was crazy, not me. Since doing that work, I believe that I deserve to be treated better and I'm finding men who DO treat me better.

Leah
TheMiracleJournal.com

9 THE KEY TO TURNING THE CRUMBS INTO CAKE

By now you are probably reading furiously trying to get to the answer. That's okay. I'm getting there, LOL! I love it and I'm excited to share this with you. The key to turning the crumbs into cake is you. You are the key. You are what stand between the crumbs and the cake, your understanding and acceptance of you.

"What does the mean?!?!" you are screaming. "This doesn't make any sense," you are yelling. I know, I know. Just hang in there, and it will become clear soon enough.

You are the key. You, the person, under all the layers and masks, are the key to changing your life. Understanding who you are and accepting who you are is the key. When you look in the mirror and can smile and tell yourself, "I love you," you will be in the right place and no longer willing to accept crumbs.

Truth #1 - You are Worthy

At some point in your life you may have been told or it was implied that you are worthless or unworthy of loving relationships. It may have been the way you looked, your personality, or your choices that made it feel like people rejected you. You may have always felt rejected or it may have happened in recent years.

No matter what you did or do, it just doesn't seem to be enough. But the truth is, you are enough. This may be hard to grasp, say, or accept but this is something you have to believe to move forward. Accept this truth. How? Because you are here. You are unique. You are wonderfully made. You are you. That is enough.

Perhaps you are not all that convinced of your worth. What would convince you? What would make you believe? Consider the fact that you made it into this world against all odds. There were millions of sperm fighting to connect with the egg in your mother's womb, but you made it. You made it through the incubation process and the birthing process. You made it through infancy and toddlerhood; both are two potentially dangerous times in a person's life. You made it through childhood and the high school years. You made it!

There is no other person on the planet like you, no one with your fingerprint or voiceprint. There is no one with your character or exact personality. There is no one with your experiences or knowledge. There is no one like you. You are a rare find, a unique pearl, and there will never be anyone else like you in the world.

I think we lose site of our specialness because we compare or were compared to others in the world. But it is a mistake to compare ourselves to others because like I said before; there is no one like you. We are all unique for a reason. Honestly if we were all the same, the world would be pretty boring. There would not be wonderful discoveries, art, fashion, food, and all the other wonderful things the unique people of the world have created. You just have to look deeper and embrace your special imprint in the world. Your difference makes you worthy and it is all so very beautiful!

Truth #2 - You are Beautiful

Now don't throw this book down yet. You really are beautiful, even if you do not see it on the outside. Even if you cannot see past your too big eyes, nose, hips, breasts, or feet, you are still beautiful. You are a woman, so you are beautiful. Do whatever it takes to find that beauty.

What did people say about you as a little girl? What is your best feature? These are the things you can focus on until you come to a complete acceptance of every part of you as beautiful. You will get there. Take time to make yourself pretty. Experiment with your hair and makeup. Try out new clothes that flatter your natural shape. Do it for you and not for anyone else.

If you need to, why not get a makeover at the mall or enlist your fashion-forward friends for help. Make sure your new look is a natural enhancement to your features. You may want a new haircut or style, new clothing style, new glasses or contacts. Whatever you do to enhance your beauty, make sure you are comfortable with the change. But remember the change will only last if you believe you are beautiful on the inside.

To begin you will start with just one day a week then progress, as time goes on, do more days. Look in the mirror and admire your best feature. Tell yourself you are beautiful. Wrap your arms around your body and squeeze. Look into your heart and see the beauty there. Push out all the other thoughts for 15 minutes a day and keep adding time to focus on all the beauty inside of you. Meditate and positively focus on your beauty

Truth #3 You are Lovable

"Here we go again," you might be thinking. What is she talking about? Everyone knows I am the least lovable person in the world. If I were so lovable then why am I stuck here on the floor picking up crumbs? The fact of the matter is, every breathing person is lovable and that includes you. Remember when I said we are made up of energy? Remember when I said love is energy? When the two of you meet you become lovable, despite what other people say or think.

One thing to remember is people project feelings about themselves off on other people. So if you were raised by or are around people who feel unlovable, they are going to project their feelings off on you. They want you to absorb their misery so they don't feel so lonely.

Unfortunately, as children, our parents may have issues and low self-esteem that is projected on to us. Their inability to affirm our lovability causes self-doubt and we seek ways to prove we are lovable. But if you don't have it inside or believe you are lovable, you open yourself up to destructive experiences and behaviors. It took a while for me to believe I am lovable. I had to see myself through the eyes of the Creator and begin saying affirmations to remind myself that I am, in fact lovable.

One technique I used was to use the word "loveable1" as my password for my work computer. I had to type it in at least 10 times a day to access my computer, so I was planting the seed each day in my mind. It was becoming a habit and a new groove was being impressed in my brain everyday. It was a form of self-hypnosis and it worked. Now I know I am lovable and even if I begin to doubt because things aren't going the way I want it at the moment, I shake off the feeling and believe again.

You can use this same technique to change your beliefs about who you are. Every month or every three months use a different word for your computer password. You can build a new and more solid foundation for your life and acquire new ways of thinking about who you are. This will make you a more powerful woman who will no longer accept crumbs.

Holding Out for Better: Tapping Into Your Power

You know the 10 behaviors women accept or allow that place them in a crummy situation. Though it is clear, it can be challenging to change. What can you do differently and why should you be the one to make changes? I mentioned before that it's up to you because you are the one reading the book and seeking answers. The real reason is because you as a woman are the relationship expert. There is really no way around this. It's in our DNA. We are relational and we create the atmosphere in all relationships. You can see this as crippling or as powerful. Hopefully you will choose the latter and begin embracing that power. With this power you can change the course of your relationships and life. But I warn you to use this power only for good.

It is fair to state that domestic violence knows no boundaries. In fact, it can affect anyone from very poor to very wealthy, illiterate to highly educated and affect all ethnic groups. No one is spared! Smart women are just as much exposed to batterers as their less educated counterparts. The fact that she is smarter will bring more shame onto herself because she assumes that her professional success can be transferred onto her personal life. She will then try to "fix" the relationship to be the "perfect partner."

She may have never been exposed to domestic violence and therefore can't identify the warning signs or maybe this type of relationship is the only type she's ever known. Maybe she is the co-dependent type or has low self-esteem or doesn't have any boundaries etc. Most importantly, the abusive man doesn't show his true colors early on in the relationship. In fact, he is "the perfect mate," therefore she falls for him deep and hard. But most abusers do not stay on this perfect behavior for very long and if she gives it enough time to really find out who he is the truth will start unraveling.

Looking at his interaction with his family, his friends, her family and her friends, and running a background check will offer additional information. She must look for some warning signs such as: is he extremely jealous, possessive, or controlling? Too often she sees the signs but choses to ignore them or she excuses his bad behaviors because she hopes he will change. She is now hooked and loves him, which makes things more complicated. Besides he already knows her weaknesses because she freely shared them with him early on in the relationship. He will use that to manipulate her and to keep the control over her.

One out of four women in this country will experience some forms of abuse during the course of her life time.

Lise Descoteaux

Section III

10 THE 10 CRUCIAL STEPS TO GETTING THE CAKE

Finally, we get to the **10 Crucial Steps to Getting the Cake You Deserve**. The following 10 Steps are about behavior modification. They are the opposite of the 10 crummy behaviors we talked about earlier. Let's get to it!

Crucial Step 1 - Never Accept Late Phone Calls

He calls you late at night expecting you to answer, be there, or entertain him. It annoys you and makes you feel taken for granted. Plus, he is not always there for you and doesn't always answer or return your calls. It's pretty much a one way street.

To change this behavior in your current guy simply do not answer the telephone after a certain time you set for yourself. This may be 9pm or later. It will be hard to let the call go to voicemail or let the text message go unanswered. You may be afraid of what he will think. He might get angry or he might get worried. If you want to know if it is an emergency, you can listen to the voicemail and read the text message. This will help you know if it is the same type of call or a real emergency. The next day when he calls simply tell him you were asleep.

Continue the pattern and he will change. The key is to not make excuses and not to apologize. You are doing what is best for you. You may be wondering if you should explain what and why you are doing this. The short answer is no. Explaining or being logical is for men. Women simply go by their feelings. Men cannot argue with feelings like they can with logic. They cannot argue with emotions because they just... are. Keep this in mind anytime you have the urge to argue with men. Trust me you will lose every time, even if you win the argument. You will lose self-respect and his heart.

If this is a new guy you are working with, you have the opportunity to start off on the right foot. It is crucial to set the tone in the beginning by setting a standard that will make any future encounters with this person pleasing to you.

You meet a guy at an event, church, office, or online. He likes you and wants to get to know you. In your first conversation he is charming and tells you how beautiful he thinks you are. You are full of smiles and accept his complements gracefully. He asks if he can talk on the phone and he gives you his number. You say yes, that would be nice and take his number. You write your number on the back of the paper or card he gave you and say you prefer if he calls you. As you are handing him the paper look him in the eyes and say you would love to hear from him as long as it's before 9pm (or whatever time you choose as long as it's before 10pm).

Follow that with, "I simply must get my beauty sleep." You are smiling the entire time but very serious. The timing and follow up statement are crucial because you are setting a boundary for yourself. You are telling him your preference in advance and letting him know that you are putting yourself first. The old adage that we teach people how to treat us is true. In this situation, you are teaching the guy who wants to get to know you that you have boundaries and self-respect. You are teaching him that you only accept cake and will never be a crumb snatcher. Do you get it? I hope so. After this exchange you let him have the paper with your number on it then change the subject or simply say goodbye and leave if it's that time.

A word about texting. It is a new trend for people to text about everything. It seems relationships are built around texting and the two parties are completely comfortable with it. However, in my opinion it, until a real relationship is established, texting should not be the primary way you communicate with a new guy you want to get to know. Now if you are not really serious about him and don't care, text until your heart is content. But if you want to get to know the guy because you like his qualities and think he'd make a good companion, boyfriend, or husband, do not fall into the texting trap. You will set yourself up to be a play thing and he will never be really serious about you.

Crucial Step 2 - Never Accept Excuses For Tardiness

Your guy is always late. He shows up when he wants to and it drives you crazy. You have missed weddings, dinner reservations, movie previews, and just about every important event in your life because he is always late.

This is embarrassing, annoying, and is a serious problem. If you are a late person yourself this probably doesn't bother you or doesn't matter. But if you care about getting somewhere on time or want him to show up before your dinner is ice cold, then it does matter. Your time is being disrespected. But what do you do?

With your current guy, you have options. You can stop seeing him or simply be late for something that matters to him. Again, give no explanation and make no excuses. Simply take your time and take it for granted that he wants to get someplace on time. It will make him angry but he will get the message. That is all you are trying to do. If he asks you why you are always late simply tell him you thought that's how he liked doing things. Tell him you feel annoyed when he is always late and that you feel your time is not important.

If this is a new guy who has asked you on a date you set the tone in the beginning. During your phone conversations, you want to tell him you like a guy who is on time and does what he says he will do. You are not demanding and don't give him the 3rd degree about his behavior.

If he shows up late, you simply do not go with him. Take your date clothes off and put on your casual clothing then relax with a movie, a magazine, or your knitting project. When he finally comes tell him you can't go because he said he would be there by a certain time and he wasn't. He can schedule another day and time (at least three days from that time) if he'd like.

Wish him a good night and close the door. The next time he will be on time because you have stood by your word. You have shown self-respect. If he is a true gentleman and a good guy he will respect your feelings and understand you mean what you say going forward.

Crucial Step 3 - Never Accept Forgotten Birthdays and Holidays

Traditionally, birthdays and holidays are a special time to show the one you love (or at least want to impress) how much you care. Sure you can do that any day of the year, but those days are either exclusively yours, like your birthday, or a time you get to celebrate with the world or at least your corner of the world.

You have to admit, we as women are pretty sentimental. Celebrations have meaning and we like the people in our lives to help us celebrate. We give and want to make days like birthdays, Christmas, and Valentine's Day special for the people we love. We also want the people who love us to give and make the days special for us too. There is no rhyme, reason, or logic behind it. It just feels good and right because it brings us closer together.

So the guy in your life forgets or does not acknowledge your birthday. Did this annoy you at first? Were your feelings hurt? Did you stuff it down because you just wanted to be a part of his life? When you brought it up, did he brush it off and say sorry or it's not a big deal? If so, and it does matter to you, then you have a little problem that will not magically go away. He's not going to suddenly start remembering and celebrating your birthday and other holidays that are important to you.

As usual, you have options and as usual they do not involve talking to him. Simple action is what it takes to make your birthday and holidays wonderful. I will get to them in a few minutes but first I want to say a couple of words about how he may view these days. He, like all men, has a past. Birthdays and holidays may have been important to him at one time, but they could have been disregarded, or he could have been made to feel insignificant for one reason or another. Somewhere in his life, he decided it wasn't worth it to acknowledge these days. This has nothing to do with you. With that in mind let's move into how you can make these days special, no matter if he's on board or not.

Make a decision to celebrate your special days whether he is there to be a part of it or not. Get happy and get off your behind. Do what makes you happy and feel good. Do not put the responsibility on him to make your day wonderful. Plan your birthday party or night out with friends and go. If he asks, tell him you have plans and then leave. Come back filled with laughter and love because your close friends and/or family were there helping you celebrate.

Do the same with the holidays that matter to you. If he has an issue with Valentine's Day, let it go and don't expect anything from him. Instead, go out and buy your own flowers, candy, and gift. Empower yourself by taking responsibility for your own happiness. If he asks who gave you the flowers, just smile. You can choose to answer or not answer. He doesn't have to know what you did for yourself. In fact, if you have always wanted to receive flowers, start buying them or sending them to yourself. You decide how often, just do it enough to fill the longing you have for something beautiful. When you handle this with grace and love, you may find he comes around. He will want to get in on the action to make you happy and be the reason you smile.

If you are dating a new guy, have the conversation about how you feel about birthdays and holidays. He will let you know his thoughts about it. You can make a choice not to date him because he does not celebrate those days. They are important to you so you should not settle with someone who does not acknowledge what's important to you.

I was in a toxic relationship in my 20's. My boyfriend at the time was on steroids (I didn't know it) and had some really crazy breakdowns. During the last breakdown that I saw, he came after me and tried to hit me. I locked myself in my car and he punched my car about ten times. I drove off and never looked back. Did I mention I was in New Jersey visiting his family and lived in Atlanta? I got on the road at that time, left my suitcase at his parents' house and never talked to the guy again. I promised myself that I was worth more than a guy who wanted to hit me and bring me down in some way. I told myself that I would never take physical abuse from any relationship and so as soon as it got close to that point, I left and never returned. I really loved him but he wasn't going to change and I was not going to be anyone's punching bag. EVER.

Stacie C., Atlanta, GA

Crucial Step 4 - Never Accept Disrespectful Language

Profanity. Some love it. Some hate it. If you are among the group of people, particularly women, who hate it, then never accept it. Don't accept the excuse that the man in our life can't help it. He can help it. He chooses not to because it's easy to say what you want and not change.

I believe profanity, the excessive torrent of words spewed out on a constant basis in the absence of any intelligent words, is a pity. It is degrading and disrespectful, especially to women. If you are looking for a true gentleman, you will not hear these words coming out of his mouth. If he regards and respects women, he will not assault your ears with profanity.

Unfortunately, women have accepted and even joined in this practice. They bring themselves down to a lower level by participating in an attempt to fit in. Of course, some do not know any better because that is how they were raised, but it is not too late to raise your standards.

So what do you do when you are in a relationship with a man who uses disrespectful language? Do you leave him? Do you pinch him every time he says a bad word? Do you sigh and roll your eyes? Or do you do nothing at all?

You can mention it to him and tell him how it makes you feel. Think about it and express it through word pictures or a simple demonstration. Men are visual so they can understand better when they see, in their mind's eye or in real life, how you feel. You can say something like, "Honey, every time I hear that word I feel like I'm being stabbed in the eye" or "Honey, every time you say that word I want to crush the family jewels with a vise grip." Say it with a smile and know you have created a word picture that will not easily leave his mind.

If you are dating a new guy that likes to pepper his words with profanity you owe it to yourself to tell him how you feel. Let him know you will not be around to listen to it in every conversation. He may promise not to do it because he likes you and wants you around but he may slip up.

Action steps to take include simply excusing yourself to go to the bathroom each time he does it. You can simply stop talking and let him realize what he is doing. You can refuse to see him again. You have options. Play around with them all and decide how long you will let him "forget." Determine your limit and stick to it. He may get upset and say you are making a big deal out of it. This is your sign to stop all communication and delete his number from your phone. He does not respect you and will not change or permanently modify his behavior to be with you. A real man will do whatever it takes to please you.

Crucial Step 5 - Never Accept Constant Sexual Innuendo

In recent years and with the proliferation of hip hop music that exploit women, there has been a rise in the level of disrespectful behavior. The most prevalent sign is the barrage of sexual comments toward and outright sexual harassment of women. Sex texting or sexting is on the rise, not just among teens, but among adults as well.

It's hard to have an intelligent conversation without there being some sexual reverence sprinkled throughout the conversation. Many men ask probing questions about body parts and favorite sexual positions to get the woman to engage in sex talk. This happens on the first date or worse during the initial conversation. If you choose to engage in this kind of talk, you send the message you are open to a sexual encounter early in the relationship.

In my dating experience, I've encountered guys who seem wonderful on the surface and claim to be respectful, turn the conversation around on a dime. One guy in particular was intelligent, a successful business owner, and a single parent. He was very attractive and obviously attracted to me. But he was like a kid in the candy store and had no filter whatsoever. He was overly aggressive and ignored my requests and attempts to talk about something more than the last time I had sex. He talked about his other conquests and bragged he was good in bed. He was sexy for sure but annoying as hell!

He, like many men who can't have their way do, accused me of being uptight and basically a prude because I did not want to talk about sex with him. We were not a good fit and I let his phone calls go to voicemail. Eventually, he stopped calling.

Had I accepted this kind of behavior from him I would have found myself in a compromising sexual position because inevitably he would have pressured me into having sex with him. Regardless of what people think, the conversations you have with people affect your mind and emotions. Trying things out just to see how it goes or fooling yourself into thinking you can handle this constant flow of information is setting yourself up for failure.

I could have let this guy's success, intelligence, and good looks blind me to his true motivations and character. It would have been easy to get caught up in his game, but I wanted more than a fling or friends with benefits status. I wanted to be more than a back pocket girl. Falling for the sex talk and letting it dominate the conversation is the fast track to sitting under the table with the crumbs. You are the easy catch and the one that is easily disregarded and thrown onto the heap with the other girls they use.

But you have options. You can set the guidelines early in the process. You can sweetly say you prefer not to discuss your private life until you've known him for at least three months. Seems like a long time but you know how quickly it goes by. If he's as wonderful as he claims to be, he will wait and respect your wishes.

You can choose what you listen to and the kind of conversation you have. You deserve to be respected and treated like a lady. Of course, you do not have to be overly sensitive. If a man compliments you in a tasteful manner, say, "thank you." If he says he loves your dress, your hair, or your smile, that is not over the top behavior. But if he begins talking about your luscious lips, beautiful breasts, gorgeous hips and butt, then your red flags should start waving furiously in the wind.

If he touches himself frequently or is getting an obvious erection and is not trying to hide it you might want to find the nearest exit. If he talks about how passionate he is and how much he loves giving massages, that is a clue he is only thinking about sex. If he starts telling you all the things he wants to do to you, run! These are not conversations you have with a person you just met or barely know (less than three months).

Freedom of speech is our right, but it does not outweigh the personal right to a harassment-free life. Use your power, command the cake through you behavior and skip out on the guy that peppers his conversation with sexual comments, innuendo, and sexual overtures. You do not have to be nice and listen to this nonsense. Stand up, step out, and find someone worthy of your time and attention.

As a teen and up until about a year ago, I allowed myself to be in toxic relationships with males. Then I believed that I was only good for sex and tried to make what I was doing okay by saying that it was all men want anyway, so I was just giving it to them so they wouldn't take it again. I didn't love myself and I certainly didn't know any better.

My husband and I repeatedly cheated on one another and lived as if it were normal although we didn't like being cheated on. I stayed with my husband at first because I didn't think anyone else would want me, damaged goods. So I settled and remained in that toxic relationship. However, I have learned to love myself in spite of my sexually traumatic past, and I know that my value is not in between my thighs. My husband and I have agreed to genuinely work out our issues not because we now have 3 children but because we want a healthy relationship.

L. Writes
"My Heart Speaks..."
http://www.Lariewrites.com

Crucial Step 6 - Don't Accept Dates At Home Until You are an Exclusive Couple

When you first meet a guy who says he likes you, he makes a date with you. You go out to dinner and a movie or some other outing. But pretty soon he starts hinting at wanting to taste some of your cooking. He might say he's running low on funds but still wants to see you, so you invite him to your place or you go to his for a romantic home-cooked meal. The next thing you know, one of those two places is where you end up all the time. You settle into a routine and rarely, if ever, go out anymore.

Why is this a problem? What's wrong with having dates at home instead of going out? How is this detrimental to your relationship? More importantly, how is this settling for crumbs?

The problem with dating or staying at home more than going out is you set yourself up to be taken for granted. You also set yourself up to move the relationship faster than is healthy for a solid foundation to be built. Home dates make a man comfortable and makes him assume he doesn't have to spend money on you to get your attention or prove his worthiness. If you are doing all the cooking and nurturing you are not concerned about what he's doing. Pretty soon you are playing house. You give him a key to make it more convenient for him to go in and get settled or to fix something. He gives you a key so you don't have to wait for him to get through traffic or stop by the local restaurant and pick up something to eat.

The entire scenario makes you too easy to conquer and once a man has conquered you, there is no challenge left. You become a prize to put on the shelf and take down whenever he wants you. Of course this is a worse case situation. But if you have no sense of self-worth or boundaries this could easily become the situation you find yourself in. It becomes a crummy situation.

Another problem with dates at home instead of out is it becomes too easy to get sexually involved to early. With you both feeling comfortable sitting on the sofa watching TV or a movie, you sit close and cuddle. He says the right things to you or caresses your skin. Kissing moves into necking or petting which moves into intercourse before you know it.

You may think this is what you want, but in reality you may have wanted to wait until you at least know his mother's first name. Sex too early muddies the waters of the relationship. After having sex you do not think clearly or objectively about the man you are dating. Problems come up over and over again because of expectations. In his mind, you belong to him and are subject to his domination. This may seem extreme, but the male nature dictates this kind of behavior.

If you are not in the mindset to be conquered or dominated it causes problems. He continues to come over and you have expectations that he is going to get serious about you or at least take charge of the relationship and steer it in the direction of marriage. Often this is not the case and you become a convenient sex partner. This too, is a crummy situation.

The last problem with dates at home instead of going out is money. Very little is being spent, or as I like to say, invested, in you. When you date at home, he's off the hook to prove he can and is willing to be a provider. You probably aren't expecting trips to Milan, but you would like to know he can and will pay for a decent meal once a week or so. You may not think it's a big deal, but it really is. You may feel like a gold digger but you are not.

You are worthy of having the man who is spending so much time, or I should say taking so much of your time, to prove that he has something to offer you. Nice words, otherwise known as flattery, promises, etc., are not the same as taking you out, taking you on trips, or buying you quality gifts (think jewelry, clothing, electronics). I know it sounds horrible or even old fashioned, but it is not that way.

Men are the ones who have to prove their worth. They have already decided you are worthy simply because they asked you out in the first place. They are under the gun to prove they are worthy of you. You are not obligated to do them any favors but are required to test their worthiness. Please get this point.

You are required to test their worthiness if you do not want to end up with a crummy guy and be in a crummy situation. His willingness to take you out on dates and spend money on you is one of the ways he should prove himself. If he makes excuses by saying he never has any money, he is always too tired, he wants to only eat your food, he doesn't have transportation (or decent transportation) to take you anywhere, then he is not worthy of you. If he never takes the initiative to plan a date or a trip or do anything special for you, he is not worthy of you.

A man who is truly worthy of you and really likes you as a person will do whatever it takes to make you happy. You have to be willing to step back and evaluate the situation clearly then decide if this is the person you want to invest so much of yourself and your time to. You may have to throw back a lot of fish before you catch the best one, or you may have to let a lot of buses go by before the right one comes along, but your life depends on it.

You have the information and the choice to make sure any guy that comes into your life is worthy of you. Watch the signs and trust your heart and intuition. If it doesn't feel right take time away from the guy who just wants to sit at the house and watch movies.

Make yourself busy every night of the week, even if it's just to wash your hair or do laundry. Pull back and see if he sticks around and offers to take you out. You have a right to start the dating process over if this person is someone you really like. The time away will let you know his motives and character. Use it to evaluate him and decide if you want to live with the crumbs or be offered cake.

I had a toxic relationship at age 26 to 28. (I am now age 56. I have three college degrees and at that time had two of them.) I taught at a university and fell in love with a man 5 years younger than me, who worked with me in the language lab. He was an extremely gorgeous young man from India. We ended up having the most passionate affair of my life, making love several times a day, every day. Eventually, his true colors of control came out. We gained a reputation of being not only madly in love but mad at each other and often this broke out into violence. Once I even went to work with heavy makeup covering a black eye, and a cast from a broken foot! I wrote in my book:

The adrenaline high and passionate make-ups work in the beginning. Then, slowly, your self-esteem lowers into a deep abyss. Then you start to feel you deserve being hit and verbally abused. You become abusive yourself, and it turns into a cycle until one day you wake up and think, "How did this happen—to me?"

So, how did I escape? I took a job overseas teaching English in Saudi Arabia!

Stella Vance
Dancing with Duality: Confessions of a Free *Spirit*

Crucial Step 7 Never Accept His Temper, Rages, or Extreme Sensitivity to Everything

Your guy has a temper or is prone to sulking when his fragile feelings are hurt. The smallest things set him off, but you think it's cute at first. He defends you against other guys and you feel safe and wanted. But pretty soon he turns his temper on you. At first, he shouts but quickly apologizes and makes the excuse he's had a bad day. You let it go, but it happens again over something trivial. If he's not flying off the handle, he's in a corner sulking and making everyone miserable.

What is this really about? Why would a full grown man be prone to temper tantrums? My observation over the years and from personal experience, I've found that men with temper tantrums have never fully matured. They were allowed to throw tantrums in their families and did not learn how to resolve problems any other way. They may have seen this behavior growing up and think it's the way to handle issues. Some men are taught this behavior from fathers, uncles, or peers as a way to get what they want. Anger issues consume them, so they act out aggressively.

Some men are extremely violent because of their environment and have no correction from responsible adult males. So what happens when you run into a guy like this? Despite his temper tantrum, he can be very charming, which is the side he shows you. He says all the right things and makes you feel like a princess. You are the world to him and the relationship progresses. He has a way of manipulating you that you can't put your finger on. He finds out all about you by asking probing questions. You answer them because they seem harmless, when in fact they become ammunition for future arguments. But you are blind to this because he's so nice and giving you the attention you crave.

Over time the chink in Prince Charming's armor begins to show. One little misstep releases an avalanche of words that shock you, followed by a quick apology. He may even send you flowers or bring you your favorite candy. As time goes on, his outburst escalate and become more frequent if you have not recognized the signs, listened to your intuition, and gotten away from him. Let's hope you haven't had sex with him because he becomes more venomous and possessive after he's conquered you.

What seemed like harmless temper tantrums is the precursor to full-blown physical, psychological, and verbal abuse. All the signs of an abusive male cannot be covered in this book, but are important to know and understand. I can share signs to look out for in the person you are dating. Trust your intuition most of all. It will not lie to you because you have an inner safety detection device that goes off if you are in a situation that could be harmful to you.

Signs he's an abusive person
- He treats service staff horribly (i.e. scowls, argues, puts down, name calling, etc.)
- He has nothing good to say about anyone, ever
- He hates children
- He hates women (except you, of course)
- He talks about how everyone has wronged him

I was in a relationship with an abusive guy for almost two years. It started out lovely and it felt like he was the man of my dreams. He said all the right things, was heavily involved in church activities, smiled all the time, and made me feel like

I was the center of his world. But a few things happened that should have been red flags.

Before I get to them let me share my state of mind when I met him. I was feeling the sting of rejection from a man that I thought I loved with all my heart and wanted to be married to. This man basically rejected me (I couldn't see it any other way) and left without any assurance we'd be together. I was feeling lonely, desperate, and needy. The new guy picked up on this and befriended me.

I was a part of the single's ministry and so was he. I shared a lot with the group so everybody new my situation as a single mom who just wanted someone to love me. I basically had a sign on my forehead that said take advantage of me because I'm vulnerable.

This abuser showed interested in me and we began to date. The red flags that began to wave gently then furiously in the wind included several things he said and did. He said he didn't like kids, but I had two kids; my oldest really like him and tried to befriend him but I saw signs that he was irritated when she came around; however I ignored it. I figured if he liked me he would grow to like my kids.

The next sign was a sob story he told me about his dad leaving and a lame story he wrote about a bird that was meant to touch my heart since I was a writer. He told me he gave bible studies to various women in his apartment building, but they all turned out to be horrible people. He never had anything nice to say about women, especially those who did not cater to him.

One day he showed up at my house for a date in tattered clothes and shoes which was very different from the clean cut look he had at church. I ordered food and he proceeded to eat most of it and didn't offer to pay for any of it. His car was filthy and always having mechanical problems that frustrated him immensely. He looked for and got sympathy from me about it while sitting in on my couch waiting for the car to cool down. Because I felt sorry for him, I gave him a hug and let him kiss me.

In the end of that evening, he had taken advantage of my kindness and forced himself on me. He date raped me. He convinced me that WE had sinned and needed to get married so we would not continue living in sin. I agreed and we got married. I was in shock and didn't understand that it was date rape until years later.

He oozed crumminess and toxicity. From day one, he was a Dr. Jekyll/Mr. Hyde and went from super nice to mean and abusive. He apologized at first but then each incident of abuse ended up either being my fault or one of my kids' fault. We could never do anything right and it wasn't until he started beating on my son that I knew I had to get out before I killed him.

The overly sensitive guy

This man's feelings are hurt about everything. You can barely have a conversation without his feelings getting bruised. It feels like you have to walk on eggshells around him because the slightest thing you say will have him sulking in the corner. The overly sensitive guy is really a manipulator and possibly a narcissist. Everything is about him and everyone is either out to get him or should be worshipping at his feet.

How did he get this way? Partly because he was either excessively petted growing up or neglected and now is trying to over compensate. He has emotional issues beyond your control, but he tries to control everyone with his hypersensitive feeling by making them feel guilty. Being with this kind of person is draining and taxes your resources, be it emotional, physical, or financial.

By the time you leave the relationship you will have to go into recovery to regain your sense of self. It will be hard to recognize a "normal" person or man because you've been overwhelmed with the overly sensitive guy.

Signs to look out for include:
- The silent treatment
- Feeling manipulated in every conversation
- Feeling guilty for saying how you feel
- Being told you hurt his feelings when you said this or that
- He cries during disagreements

I was married to the overly sensitive guy and couldn't say two words without it being misinterpreted. He took offence at everything I said that didn't agree with his way or thinking. If I wasn't praising him 24/7, even when he was doing something unethical, dishonest, and downright shady, he was offended.

Why didn't I know about this before I married him? I think it's because I wanted to see the good in him and at first he said and did all the right things. How would he know the right things to say and do? Well because I shared all my hopes and dreams with him too early. I poured out my guts to him, just laid it all out on a silver platter for him to pick through, decipher, and plan.

I made it easy for him to be my knight in shining armor when in fact he was simply a cad. He was offended because I expected him to keep his word and be what he claimed to be. But that is not the kind of material he was made of. He was nothing like he claimed to be. He was a fake. Being found out was hard for him.

Once the wool that was over my eyes was ripped away, I had no choice but to see him for who he really was. So I questioned him. I saw that in reality, he was more like a homeless man looking for a place to crash or a chameleon trying to change his colors to take advantage of the situation. His sensitivity was really about fear of losing what he wanted to keep. He wanted to feel like he was the man and in control, but the reality was he didn't know how to control himself.

The weaker a guy feels the more he will try to exert control over someone else's life. He has never learned self-control so he exhibits all the signs of a spoiled child under pressure. He pouts, shouts, and practically holds his breath. With more resources at his disposal, he is able to do more damage. He has learned more words so he can use them to manipulate you. He has learned how to read people so he can read your expressions and know which buttons to push you over the edge.

He hears when you ask for something or make requests; the small things that make you happy, and then he does the opposite to frustrate you. He uses your natural mothering instinct to his advantage by letting tears well up in his eyes. When you finally stand up for yourself tell him how awful he is being to you. He turns it all around on you to make you feel guilty. I lived with this day after day until I decided I had enough. I begged for counseling and for change but I learned the hard way that people, especially men, don't change because you want them to change. Instead, they become more stubborn and remain resolute in their crummy behavior.

I often wonder what I could have done differently. Looking back I see I could have taken things a lot slower. Rushing into a relationship just because a guy liked me is not a good reason to trust him. I could have insisted he prove himself. I could have asked more questions and set boundaries. There is a lot I could have done differently, but I think the biggest thing I could have done was to be in a healthy state of mind.

Relationships don't start out as toxic. My high school sweetheart was so great in the beginning. Smart, good looking and I thought I was lucky.

Slowly he started hanging out with the wrong crowd and invited drugs and alcohol in. That is when things became toxic. The more we argued, the more his temper seemed to spiral out of control, until finally he turned to mental and physical abuse. The only reason I broke free from that relationship was because of an empowering best friend, and the distance that I got from going to a different college than him.

Rose T.

Crucial Step 8 - Never Accept Pressure to Have Sex When You Want Intimacy

Too many men would have you thinking that everybody is doing it, so they pressure you into having sex when all you really want is intimacy. It becomes a battle of wits to see who will win. But why should it be a battle for anything?

Unfortunately, women give in to having sex too early or too often because they think it is the only way to get intimacy. But men do not feel or get intimacy from sex when they are not emotionally invested in you. They just get a physical release and you are left feeling empty.

I have experienced being pressured to have sex from the time I was sixteen or so. Guys would say all kinds of things to get me to have sex with them. This was especially so if we did a lot of kissing and necking. Like normal guys, they got excited and wanted release, but I wasn't having it. I wasn't ready for it, so I said no. I did not feel comfortable doing that, plus I was saving myself for that special someone and marriage.

But I got older and feeling my prospects dwindling with each passing year, I soon gave in to the pressure. I was supposed to be getting married to the guy so it was okay, right? But I was violating my own policy because the pressure was more than I could handle since I moved in with him. That was a mistake on my part, so I put myself in the situation. In the end, we didn't get married so I felt bad about it for a long time.

Looking back, I see that I didn't want sex so much as I wanted intimacy and closeness that didn't involve intercourse. I wanted a connection with him that was on the heart level. I wanted to feel safe and get to a place where there was a true soul to soul connection. To be as close to a person as you can possibly be is what I wanted to experience. It would be the glue and the lasting connection a man and woman could have.

I wanted to feel unconditional love without having to prove it through sex. But I confused this by thinking having sex would bring the intimacy I wanted. The after effect of sex was nice but it didn't last as long as the intimacy would. I was feeling guilty because I was doing something I promised myself I would not do. So all I got was a temporary high and guilt feelings for days and weeks after the encounter. Not exactly the feeling of intimacy.

When women trade the lasting intimacy they really want for the temporary ecstasy of sex they get, it can leave a hole in their soul. Often women cover it with more sex or they emotionally eat. They do whatever it takes to fill the void.

Sex vs. Intimacy: How to Get What You Really Want

So how do you get intimacy instead of trading it for meaningless sex? It seems simple enough but it can be difficult if you do not have a solid foundation of self-love and a clear view of what you want for your life.

The first step is setting a policy for yourself to say no to all sexual advances. Do not put yourself in the situation where your senses can be compromised. Close encounters set you up for failures so deep throat kissing, fondling, and necking are all dangerous for you. In fact, make it your business to get to know a guy for longer than three months before you even let him kiss you on the lips. That seems extreme but it will weed out a lot of pretenders.

The guy with staying power who consistently respects your

policies and becomes a true friend is what you want. That is not to say every guy that can handle your policy is worth getting involved with. You have to watch the other signs as well. By implementing a time policy, you empower yourself. Intimacy is not about depriving him because you can be sure a selfish guy, who is only out for one thing, will say you are doing just that. He will pressure you to give in and violate your policies.

The first time sex comes up, you state the policy and ensure it is for your personal well-being and has nothing to do with him. It would be true because it really has nothing to do with him. You are empowering yourself to remain clear and present because you need to remain focused on what's important in your life.

You want to maintain a mind and heart that is free from morning after guilt, self-loathing, and regrets. You want to build intimacy so when you do have a sexual encounter he is touched more deeply because he knows you and loves you. You will be happier with waiting and so will he if he is a quality man.

To get the intimacy you want, be empowered to withstand any pressure a guy may put on you.

Do two things:
1.   Set you personal policies and stick with them
2.   Recognize the signs a guy uses to pressure you

Signs include:
- He says he is a very passionate person and just wants to show you
- He says he loves giving massages and would like to give you one
- He says he will get blue balls, which is very painful, if he doesn't have sex
- He is going to war and wants to be with you before he goes away to face death
- He tells you over and over again that you are so sexy
- He wants to come over and just hold you at night
- He talks about your body parts
- He asks you about you past sexual encounters
- He says you have gone too long without and must be feeling horny

All these are signs he wants to have sex with you and hopes you will give him the go ahead. Some of the lines are blatantly about him but others are disguised as concern for you. But they all go against your personal desire for intimacy. The dictionary defines intimacy as a close, familiar, and affectionate personal relationship.

Closeness can rarely be achieved within a few hours or few weeks. It takes time, many conversations and experiences to become close. There is, of course, artificial closeness. It is when two people spend, what seems like, every waking hour together. They do activities and maybe work together, but that does not translate into closeness.

Intimacy is about mutual discovery and understanding each other. It's about both people being vulnerable and sharing and accepting. That cannot be achieved in a world wind romance even though it sounds nice. But if you want intimacy, follow the two steps: set your policy and watch the signs.

Crucial Step 9 - Never Accept Invisibility

Your guy is always busy with work, community activities, church, or some other important project. It seems the only time he pays any attention to you is when he wants or needs sex. When you want to talk he's preoccupied with TV, sports, texting, etc. He may speak to you in the morning on the way to work and even then it's only to ask if you feel like having sex tonight. You sigh and say you guess so. "Good!" he says and walks out with a spring in his step.

This scenario is all too common in many households today. But it's not just in married households but also in the dating world. It's not uncommon for women to wait by the phone hoping the guy, who was so into them, will call and ask them out or just have a conversation.

Everything started out beautifully. He saw you then approached you and told you how beautiful and smart you are. He spent time with you and showered you with attention, great conversation, and affection. You enjoyed every moment and looked forward to his phone calls, visits, and text messages. He made you feel wanted and special.

You didn't have to lift a finger to beckon him because he was there, then one day he doesn't call. His texts are sporadic and he doesn't ask to come visit. You don't hear from him for a week then he resurfaces and talks to you like nothing happened. He tells you he's missed talking to you, and you tell him you missed him too.

He's gone again and now it becomes two weeks, even three weeks before he pops up again. This is confusing and hurtful because you don't understand what's happening. Your feelings are hurt and you try to live a normal life in spite of the void he's left. What's odd is he shows up like clockwork. He's in and out of your life like a revolving door. You find yourself waiting for a call or text.

You call him and leave messages and text him, but he doesn't respond for hours or even days. You think it's something you've done but what you don't realize is you have become the Back Pocket Girl. You are the one he can keep in his back pocket for convenience. You are always there for when he needs an emotional fix. If you were just a jump off or one night stand, he might come around more frequently.

Usually the Back Pocket Girl is the woman he's not sleeping with. You are the good woman who waits for him to come to his senses. He loves the thought of you and can see himself with you, but he's not ready to commit yet. He's still got some playing to do and is trying to work out his "issues." You are the invisible, but constantly reliable, girl he can pull back into his life when all the other options have fizzled out.

The only one who benefits in this kind of relationship is him. You are left holding the bag or the short end of the stick. You are left wondering where you stand but I can tell you where you stand... in his back pocket.

A Note about being the Back Pocket Girl

Who can see their back pocket? We all know it's there, but we can't really see it. It might contain a wallet or a cell phone or even a stick of gum or folded up piece of paper or photo. You only pull it out when you need it. Sometimes it may be forgotten and will go through several washes until he pulls it out one day. He'll unfold it and though it's damp, he will recognize it and a light bulb will go off in his head. He'll get a warm fuzzy feeling and decide to follow up.

When he thinks about you he'll call or text. He'll say he's missed you and wants to see you. You may be so overjoyed that you forget how invisible you've been up to that moment. You can stay invisible or you can come out into the light and show yourself. How do you do this? How do you stop being invisible? In this case you let him know you will no longer be available. You tell him not to call or text you anymore because you deserve more than infrequent phone calls and dates. You deserve more than being the Back Pocket Girl and you've decided to move on.

You come into the light by dating other men and keep dating until you find the one who sees the value you know you have. You will continue the cycle of invisibility for as long as you allow it to happen. You deserve more than crumbs of attention. You deserve to be the center of attention, which is like eating a delicious slice of cake!

Crucial Step 10 - Never Accept Last Place

It seems you are never a top priority. Whenever you want time alone with him or attention, you get pushed aside. You have to wait until everyone else's needs are met before you are even considered. He says it's because he's important or he's a nice guy and cannot help being there for others. He says you should be grateful to have such a generous guy for a boyfriend/husband. All you feel at this point is resentful. You are tired of being on the back burner and want more.

To accept last place is how you disrespect yourself. A man who says he loves you and/or has married you should never make you his last priority. You are part of his life and deserve top spot. Sure he has a job/career, extended family obligations, and hobbies that are important to him, but they should never come before you.

If this is happening there is a disconnect somewhere that must be examined. Perhaps he has an ego that he needs stroked continuously. Perhaps something happened in the past between you that he hasn't gotten over. Maybe he feels disrespected and feels he can't get your approval. If this is happening find a way to resolve the issues.

If the problem has nothing to do with what you've done or a part you've played in this disconnect, it's up to you to find out what it is. Maybe you have been relegated to the role of doormat. If you were brought up to think you are simply a glorified servant to your spouse or mate, you should probably rethink and renegotiate your role.

When you become a timid doormat you give him permission to make you last. If you are afraid to speak up you give him permission to keep ignoring you. It's only when you are tired of being last that you will change the situation.

If you are ready, you can move from last place to first place. If you have a good man, you can change this by changing your behavior. Men respond to action and rarely words. They feel the difference when your behavior changes.

Changing your behavior may happen in several ways. You have to know your man and his patterns to affect change. You are smart and clever, so you will know what to do. If he's used to dinner at a certain time change the time or don't have it ready. If he's used to hearing from you by a certain time change the time or don't let him hear from you.

You do not have to be vindictive or dangerous but you do have to be effective and perhaps even calculating. The point is to move yourself up to the number one spot in his life. You do this by making yourself number one and bumping him down on your list of priorities.

If he cannot get with the program or refuses to give you the respect you deserve you will have to decide if he's worth keeping. That is the last resort of course, which is why I prefaced this section with knowing you have a good man. He must be worth keeping and capable of giving you cake instead of crumbs.

I've been in several "dysfunctional" relationships and one in particular. I met him in a continuing studies course while I was on the verge of separating from my husband, a man 33 years older than me whom I had been with for almost nine years. My husband really served as more a mentor than a lover, and for five of our nine years together we were not intimate: his choice, not mine.

This man, was a predator. He crept in slowly, first by being kind and available, then playful, then romantic, then laying the charm on thick. I moved in with him, as I had nowhere else to go. Soon after, I discovered what he was. He'd go hot and cold, hot and cold, confusing things with guilt trips, martyrdom, rhetorical questions, accusations. I was brainwashed. I actually became acquainted with his assistant whose mother is a family counselor and who sensed something was very off. She and another friend made the plan for me of how I was to get out of his house. I never would have believed I was ever a person this could happen to. But I was not invincible.

Emma Tai

11 YOUR NEW FUTURE SHOULD YOU CHOOSE TO ACCEPT IT

You are fearfully and wonderfully made, says the psalmist. But we don't believe that do we? We treat ourselves badly and believe all the horrible things people say about us individually and as a gender. For thousands of years we have been blamed for the state of the world because of mother Eve.

Now it seems every daughter of Eve is punished for one thing or another. Being too much of a woman, being a temptress, being too dominating, too possessive, too overbearing, too weak, too sensitive, too beautiful, not beautiful enough, too thin, too fat; but never enough.

On the worldwide stage women are victimized by the physically stronger, more powerful male. In Africa, woman are raped and mutilated in acts of war. In some Asian countries, woman are enslaved against their will in the sex trade, then bought and sold to give men sexual pleasure. Women and children are the poorest and least regarded. This has been sadly true throughout history.

Domestic violence runs rampant as mentally and emotionally weak men prey on innocent women and children. With all these issues you would think the Universe or God hates women. That is what many religions teach, some overtly and others covertly. Some biblical scholars went so far as to twist the meaning of words in the Bible during translation to keep women under control. This is unfortunate because for a male to repress the voice of women in the world is to harm himself.

The truth is, in the eyes of the Universe, in the eyes of love, women are every bit as important as men. Women bring different qualities and value to the world. I like to say, in a world of black and white that men create, women bring a tapestry of color. Women brighten the room and bring things into balance.

Learning the Recipe for the Cake You Deserve

Knowing the truth about who you are is not enough. You have to accept, embrace, and begin living this truth out in your life daily. This means developing a healthy relationship with yourself. This is the foundation of any good relationship, whether it is with a man, your family, or your co-workers. Developing a healthy sense of self sets the tone for how all your relationships will go.

Having a healthy relationship with yourself involves getting to know who you are as a person. It also involves knowing who you are. You are a person born of love. You survived the birthing process. You made it to this point in your life, hopefully without any major traumas. You are here. You were born for a purpose. It could be a small as brightening someone's day with your infectious smile or baking the best bread in town. But you have to recognize your value and your contributions to this world. It is very important no matter how small or insignificant you think it may be.

A healthy relationship with yourself looks like a great friendship. If you have a best friend you know what this is. The best friend relationship is probably a more transparent and real relationship you have. You can talk with her, laugh with her, and be supportive. You share advice and warn each other of potential danger. You know you are completely accepted in this relationship. In developing a healthy relationship with yourself, you elect to become your own best friend. You encourage yourself. You evaluate your decisions and come to the conclusion your best friend would come to. You accept yourself unconditionally, warts, big feet, bad back and all.

You laugh at yourself for the silly things you do, but you don't judge yourself harshly. You learn to soothe yourself when times are tough. You seek out companionship among women who uplift and encourage you. You remind yourself of the boundaries you've set and the choices you've decided to make. You remember the goals you have written and push yourself back on course when you veer too much to the left or right. Being gentle with yourself is probably the most important part of this development process. Loving the total package no matter how good, bad, or ugly is part of the deal too. Self-criticism is out the door and is replaced with graceful acceptance.

As you learn to develop a healthy relationship with yourself, you will see your relationship with others transform. It happens in two ways. You are more compassionate toward others and less judgmental. You do not allow others to be judgmental and critical of you. What other people say no longer matters because you do not need them to validate you. This is crucial in the dating and mating world because too often we are seeking validation from a guy. The reality is we will rarely get it the way we want it and it's not worth more than your own self-validation. I hope you get that. Another person's validation stamp is not better than your own stamp. A woman with a healthy self-image is able to filter information and responses with much better clarity than if she has a poor self-image.

Setting boundaries is crucial in dating and mating, as well as in life in general. Our personal space and preferences are important to making us feel safe and continue feeling a sense of individuality. So how do you set boundaries? What does that look and feel like? Maybe you have strong boundaries in one area, but they are weak in another area. Maybe your relationship boundaries are what need the work. They may be weak because you bought into the idea that you should be open and willing to do anything to make the other person happy so you drop all your boundaries when you are in a relationship.

Boundaries are set before you enter a relationship. They are established from a place of personal empowerment and a healthy self-image. We just talked about these two things. Boundaries are not about fear and they are not walls you put up. They are more like fences. Walls keep people out and keep you closed in. They become prisons. Fences keep unwanted danger out but you are still open to interactions and experiences with others.

Boundaries determine how you allow others to treat you. With healthy boundaries, you let people know by your body language and words they are not allowed to treat you poorly. You are able to say no to bad behavior. You say yes to safe behavior. Your happiness and well-being are just as important as the other person's in a relationship. There is no undue self-sacrifice and you do not allow anyone to pressure you into doing anything you do not feel comfortable doing.

Boundaries determine how you allow others to speak to you. Boundaries give you a voice to say what hurts your feelings or what is not acceptable. You do not allow verbal assaults, excessive criticism, or disrespectful language in your space. You have the right and courage to stop this behavior or walk away.

Healthy boundaries empower you to live your life in a way that pleases you.

Growing up in a single-parent home, I was determined to succeed where many of my predecessors had failed. As a result, I became an overachiever in many areas of my life, but I was more concerned with how my life appeared rather than what it really was. When I got pregnant at 16, I married the father of my child because I didn't want to perpetuate a cycle of single motherhood. Likewise, I didn't want my child to live with the poverty I experienced being raised by a single mother. Besides having unprotected sex, I didn't give any thought to the man I wanted to father my child or the one I would to marry. But I did make a conscious choice to remain in an emotionally abusive relationship that exhausted me physically. I eventually chose a life of peace and happiness over an image of who others thought I was.

L. Carroll
Lady L. Media
http://www.ladylmedia.com

Self-Discovery

Self-discovery is a huge part of living a life without crumbs. With a solid understanding and acceptance of who you are, there is a slim chance you will fall for crummy guys or accept a toxic relationship. "Know thyself" is a mantra all healthy and secure people live by. To know yourself is more than knowing your physical parts. It is knowing everything about who you are, from your idiosyncrasies to your temperament, to your hot spots. Of course, everyone has blind spots, but they are not detrimental and will not lead you into co-dependent or abusive relationships.

Self-discovery usually happens through self-exploration, self-education, and self-embracement.

Self-exploration

This has little to do with your physical body but more about your mental, emotional and spiritual state. Knowing your mind, personality and character is huge. Discovering what makes you YOU is empowering and liberating.

I spent a few years discovering who I am. I wanted to know what made me tick so I began to read up on personality types, took tests, and wrote in my journal. All this helped me to understand what made me ME. It was an exciting time for me. I began to understand the reasons why I enjoy certain activities, had certain mannerisms, and thought the way I did. I learned my view of the world is unique. I learned that I have certain characteristics of major people in history. This gave me hope and helped me build a new foundation of self-worth and self-acceptance.

As the years went by, I learned to accept my unique view

of life. It wasn't bad that I didn't like okra but that I loved potatoes. It was okay that I preferred one on one relationship versus being in a crowd. Solitude was good for me, whereas, spending every weekend at a party was draining. It was perfectly acceptable that I preferred books to television.

In learning about my personality I learned that I am outspoken and fairness is top of the list for me in human interaction. I also discovered my streak of humor that delights people. For years all of me seemed repressed. I was unsure, angry, and had a dark cloud over my life because I felt I could never measure up or be good enough. This set me up for accepting crummy guys. I thought any guy that paid attention to me, said the right things to me, or bought me dinner was worthy of my time. It validated me and caused me to accept crummy behavior. Of course it started out good, but time played out a different story.

Taking time to discover who I am changed how I approached relationships. Before I was like a hungry lap dog, willing to accept the crumbs dropped or thrown at me. I didn't take the time to really get to know the guy and learn about his habits, his past, or his story. I was just happy to be receiving validation. Now I take my time and because I have a stronger sense of self, I weigh the guys I date more carefully against my ideals and decide if being with him will make ME happy.

Self-exploration is a good thing. It's liberating. It is like an insurance policy against bad relationships. Because the stronger your sense of self, the stronger your resistance to toxic relationships.

Self-Education

Education is the cornerstone of liberation. I made that up myself, LOL! But really, it's true. Education is like a lottery ticket. If you have it, you always win. But I'm not speaking about education in the traditional sense. There are no classrooms or instructors to grade your work.

The education I am speaking of is the kind you get from opening your mind to learn all there is about a specific topic. This can happen by reading books, watching films, listening to a lecture, attending a seminar, or simply listening to a more experienced person.

The education that is essential for this discussion has to do with human nature and relationships; the successful kind. There are numerous books in the marketplace and libraries that discuss healthy relationships. There are different schools of thought on the subject so it is up to you to decide what resonates with you.

The learning process should fit your personality, which you discovered during the self-exploration phase. You may enjoy reading to learn, listening to learn, or watching to learn. You may need activities to really "get" the material or a combination may work for. Whatever way works for you, take full advantage of the process and information.

To remain ignorant at this point is counter-productive. You set yourself up for more failure in relationships. Self-education is crucial to moving forward successfully.

With the rise in e-books, audio books, YouTube videos, and websites, you have no excuse not to learn more about yourself and relationships.

Self-Embrace

Embracing yourself is an act of compassion. It is about giving yourself the support you need to make it through, not only the dating process, but through the ups and downs of life. When we embrace others we envelop them with love and support. We give them the space to be who they are. We make them feel safe in our arms or minds. We don't judge them or make them feel guilty for recent or past mistakes. It's all about being there without judgment.

In embracing yourself, you let go of the judgment that you have made mistakes or you failed in some way. You honor your feelings and experiences, and you learn to accept them as part of life. You learn how to embrace freedom from guilt, culture, and criticism.

Freedom from guilt is huge. Guilt is a part of every woman's life and it seems to be etched in our very moral fabric. It seems there is no way to escape it, but you can if you learn one key thing, learn this... Love.

When it comes to toxic relationships, the person to be examined is me. I have been in several toxic relationships throughout the course of my dating life. It wasn't until I had the mother of all heartbreaks that I began looking into myself. I asked the questions, why am I attracted to the same type of man? What is it that attracted me to them in the first place? How long did it take me to fall in love and what was I in love with?

When a woman is always in toxic relationships, she needs to examine herself and give herself time to change destructive patterns. She needs to be healed of past hurts and renewed in her thinking. It took me four years to acknowledge and change my desires. It is impossible to have a healthy relationship with an unhealthy person. If a woman won't submit to the process she will undoubtedly repeat the same mistakes over and over again. I can't say in two or three paragraphs what needs to be said about this situation. But the bottom line is that, the only way to a healthy relationship is to first sift through yourself, your habits, your desires, weaknesses, etc. When you have done those things first, then you will be able to determine God's will for your life... His good pleasing and perfect will!

Krishunna Pearson
The Making Of A Lady
www.makingalady.org

12 CHARACTERISTICS OF A QUALITY MAN

Now you know how to spot crummy guys and know what a toxic relationship is in more detail than you probably care to know. By now you are probably ready to know what a quality man looks like. I'm sure you want to know where to find him too. We will get into that later, but first let's look at what a quality man looks like.

I have identified at least 10 core characteristics of a quality man. I'll list them first then go into detail about them a little further down.

A quality man will be:
- ✓ Kind
- ✓ Generous
- ✓ Gentlemanly
- ✓ Attentive
- ✓ Protective

- ✓ Provider
- ✓ Balanced
- ✓ Respectful
- ✓ Spiritual
- ✓ Integrity

Notice I don't describe the kind of job he has or how attractive he should be. I don't go into his economic status or his leadership status. All of those things are relative and may or may not be a part of the equation. You want a man that treats you well and makes you feel loved and cherished.

Kindness

There is a marked difference between a kind man and one who is merely nice. Sometimes we confuse the two and think they hold equal value and weight but they don't. A nice man will tell you what you want to hear. He will appear interested in your well-being, but he is only really interested in how he looks to the outside world.

Don't get me wrong, being nice is okay, but it does not go very deep into having a quality character. It can be and is usually a mask for covering many things. Many people use the mask of niceness to hide their fears or sense of inadequacy. What does that have to do with this? A better question could be, "What happens when the mask is taken down?" What kind of man will he be? Will he treat you with kindness and respect or will he let his true colors show?

I've dated a few nice guys. They seemed to always be smiling and ready to "help" me. They had all the time in the world for me and did little things to make me feel like they were into me. But when the mask came off they were not so nice. A clue for me should have been the conversations we had and paying better attention to how they treated others. This is a big clue into whether the guy you are seeing is really kind or just wearing the nice mask.

A kind man will have compassion on everyone. They will treat the old lady on the street with care and the waiter with respect. They will speak kindly about their family and be careful with your feelings.

Generosity

A generous man is willing to give of his time, talent and resources for you. He does not hold back and is not selfish with you. He gives to causes, family, charity, and other various organizations. He may have his favorite cause or project. He offers help to those in need. He is not stingy and does not withhold what he has.

Generosity is developed in most people but there are some for which it comes naturally. You are fortunate if you find a man that is naturally giving. This characteristic is important to your relationship because it will determine how willing he is to help you now and in the future.

It is not all about money but about the time and talent he lends to the relationship. If he never has time for you or never wants to expend energy for you, drop him. But a man who gladly gives of the three elements is a keeper.

To know if he is a generous man, it is important to pay attention to what he says and does when someone asks for help. Does he make excuses? Does he get offended or angry when someone in his life needs help? Is he eager to help? Does he talk about how he's helped someone, not as a way to brag just as a normal part of conversation?

Gentlemanly

It seems in our society, chivalry is dead. What happened to the days of opening the car door, pulling the seat out for the lady, and helping her with heavy packages or picking up something she has dropped? It all seems like a distant dream and the stuff of fairytales.

But there are still men out there who are gentlemen and want to be the knight in shining armor. In fact, most men have it in them to be gentlemen. Some were trained when they were young by their parents. Others can be trained by you. But the potential has to be there. You can bring that out in a man by your behavior and expectations.

A gentleman is not born. In fact, most boys are quite barbaric and brutish. That is their nature, but the women in their lives refine them either in pre-adolescence or in early adulthood. Men are motivated by rewards, so your smile or approval is what keeps them eager to behave well.

A gentleman needs a lady to serve. Yes, it is an act of service for men so they need someone worthy. If you are not a lady or not behaving as a lady, it's time to start doing this. It will impact your relationship in a crucial way. For some women it may seem like a step backwards but it really is step up.

Being a lady is not about giving up equality or rights, it's about setting yourself up to be respected and cherished. Why should you do all the heavy lifting when there is a perfectly good man around to do it for you? Why should you get your hands dirty trying to change a tire when there are men around who will gladly do it for you? Why open the car door yourself when he could do it while you touch up your makeup in the seconds it takes for him to walk around the car to open the door?

You are the prize. You are the reason for the smile on his face. You are the reason he chooses to be generous and remain in that place of kindness. Let him be the gentleman and you be the lady.

It is in our DNA to seek out men who take care of us, serve us and make us feel secure. When you go against nature you always have a nagging feeling that something is not right. Things are off balance and it will not be right until you embrace the truth of who you are.

For many years, I lived the pattern of choosing the wrong people to allow into my heart. All the while, I was a successful entrepreneur. Being successful in business and unsuccessful in relationships is a pattern for many of us. I believe it's because of what I call "survivor work ethic." What I mean is that many of us have had painful childhood experiences. We grow up with the determination to prove our worth and value to the world, so we throw ourselves into our careers and achieve a measure of success. Sadly, though, focusing on career development allows us to shelve our pain and avoid working through the emotional scars of our painful past.

Consequently, we choose the wrong people and wind up hurt, again. I finally broke that cycle, and have been married 21 years to a good man. I'd love the opportunity to help successful women break out of that painful and lonely pattern by mining the lessons out of their painful pasts and in so doing, fixing their "chooser." As we work through our issues, we think better of ourselves, make better choices, and get better results. It's just that simple.

Rhonda Sciortino
Author, Succeed Because of What You've Been Through.
http://www.rhondasciortino.com

Attentive

No one likes to be ignored in a relationship. Unfortunately, millions of women are ignored each day. Some may be okay with it, but most hate it and wish their men would pay them attention.

An attentive man is concerned about your comfort and feelings. He asks if you need anything and asks how you are feeling if something seems off with you. He does not overwhelm you with attention so that he is in your face 24/7 but he is aware of your needs. This may look like different things in different relationships so I cannot go into specific details about what an attentive man will do for you.

In my observation of men and their behavior, an attentive man will do little things to make you feel important. He will be there when you need to talk or when you have a problem. He will hug you, hold your hand, touch your face and give you his undivided attention when you are together. If not for the entire time, he will give you at least 10-30 minutes of undivided attention during the dating process. He will rarely be distracted by something else like his cell phone, games, other women, or male friends he sees in public.

Protective

A man who is protective will make sure you are safe, not only physically but also mentally and emotionally as well. Of course when we think go a protective man we think of the physical first. We imagine being rescued from all kinds of danger from a lion in the wild to a small spider hanging from its web in the corner.

As a woman we know the value of a strong, protective

man. We want to know that when we go out we won't suffer the harassment of aggressive guys. We want to feel safe from unwanted attention and touches. Of course we can protect ourselves for the most part, but why be bothered when there is a perfectly capable man available.

In addition to wanting to feel physically safe, we want to feel safe from mental and emotional stresses. A man who will protect you from the harsh realities of life or from harsh people should get extra points. But it takes a healthy man to even recognize this important need women have.

For example, a protective man will stand in or defend his lady when her family or friends are pressuring her to be their personal whipping girl or banker. He will pull her away or at least speak up where she feels powerless to do so. He will see her working too hard and insist that she slow down or take a break. He will plan a getaway or suggest that she get away from the hustle and bustle of life. An extra special guy will make all the arrangements for a spa day or whisk her away for a weekend.

My ex husband was far from being protective. I should have gotten a clue before we were married. He left me on the side of the road to deal with the police that pulled me over to question me about the tags on my car. I was driving from a car auction where I'd just bought a used car. My ex was in the other car we drove to the auction.

A police officer pulled me over to ask me why I didn't have a license plate. I fully expected my then husband to stop when he saw what was happening to make sure everything was okay. Instead he kept going and drove on to the apartment. I was in shock and disbelief that he would do that. It was dark outside and I felt vulnerable.

When I asked him about it he said he knew I could handle

it. WTH!!! I let it go but didn't take it as a clue of the kind of guy he was. I ended up marrying him anyway much to my later regret. He turned out to be even less protective, in fact he was abusive. Had I followed my intuition and let him go, I would have probably saved myself a lot of heartache.

Protection is not always about being a brute or bodyguard to ward of the attack of male rivals. It includes keeping her from overworking, being stressed by her (or his) family, and sometimes saving her from herself. The objective is to ensure her happiness and peace of mind. He won't always be able to come to the rescue but by showing he cares about her physical and psychological well-being, he proves he is far from being a crummy guy.

Provider

You want a man who is happy to be a provider. He sees it as the manliest act in the world to provide for you. This provision is manifested from the first date and carries on throughout your dating life. If you decide to be with this man in a long-term relationship, you will see evidence of his provision.

Sure you probably make your own money and you can take care of yourself, but that is not the point. Part of a man's identity is being able to take care of the people he loves. It's in his DNA to be a provider and prove to you that he can take care of your material needs. So from the first date when he pays for the meal, he is setting himself up as a provider and proving to you that he can handle the role.

The number one need for women is security. We want to know that the man we are dating, in a relationship with, or married to, can provide for us. Just like being a provider is in his DNA, feeling secure is in our DNA. We need this sense of security because if we decide to have children by this person, we want to know he can and will take care of us.

We want to know we will survive under his care. This is because we as women are nurturers and feel an innate responsibility to make sure our children survive. They cannot survive if the man in our lives is not capable or unwilling to take care of us.

A man who is not only capable, but also willing to provide, is what you want. Let him buy you meals and pretty things. This is how he proves his manhood and exercises the provider muscle. He knows he is under scrutiny in this area and does not want to fall short.

Proving that he can take care of you is a natural process. Let it happen, but understand it does not mean you fundamentally owe him anything but a thank you. Of course you can bake him some cookies or make him a plate of food for him to eat later as a good will gesture or out of gratitude, but you are not obligated to give him anything. He is trying to win you over with his actions and prove himself worthy.

Balanced

This may seem like an odd thing to look for in a man but it is one of the things that will make or break a relationship. Balance is about putting all the activities in his life in perspective. This balance is about how he handles his time, his emotions, and his resources. Is he a workaholic? Is he an excessive spender? Is he overly sensitive, bitter, or moody? Is his relationship with his mother, sister, or aunt much too close to the point that he is like a child with her/them? Is he grossly overweight? Where does he spend most of his time?

Where do you fit in? What does he talk about excessively? All of these things matter.

A balanced man knows how to cope with life in a way that is healthy. His outlook is rational and he is not prone to excessive or radical behavior. A man that works too much or is obsessed with making more money will have very little time for you. A man who is obsessed with food and has to eat all the time will have health issues later in life.

A man who always looks for easy money or a get rich quick scheme is inherently lazy and will have you in the poor house. A man who has extreme shifts in his mood or is overly sensitive will have you on an emotional roller-coaster ride. A man who has to call his mother three times a day during the week and five times a day on the weekends will have you caught in a three-way relationship with her. You will be miserable knowing that she knows all the details of your relationship.

A balanced man is full grown and has a healthy sense of boundaries, acts in moderations, has a good sense of how to handle life without going to extremes. In essence, he is mature and has learned lessons in life that will keep him in balance.

With a balanced man, you can expect times of togetherness and separateness. You will not feel alone in the relationship. You will not feel like second place. A man of balance will have a wide range of things to talk about. He will have his emotions in check so you don't have to worry about what personality will surface from day to day. There will be no Dr. Jekyll/Mr. Hyde episodes.

Respectful

Respect is one of the greatest honors a person can receive. Women are no different in that we deserve respect from the man who claims to love us. Of course we want to be cherished, spoiled and loved but respect is the foundation of every healthy relationship.

A man who is respectful will honor your individuality, your body, and your feelings. He will treat you the way he wants to be treated because for a man, respect is the cornerstone of his life. He wants to be given the time and space to live life on his terms. He wants to be spoken to in a manner that does not demean, degrade or offend. He wants to be acknowledged as a full grown adult and not treated like a child. When a man is respectful, he is giving you room to breathe and grow and maintain a sense of self.

How does a respectful man treat you? He does not embarrass you with rude or crude behavior. He does not demand his own way all the time. He is not overbearing or dictatorial. He does not put you down, call you names, or manipulate you for selfish gain. He says please and thank you. He has manners, so that means he doesn't deliberately pass gas, burp, or scratch his private parts in front of you.

A man who is respectful will speak to you with kindness and never curse at you. He will touch your body only after he's asked or is given permission. He will not try to force you to watch or listen to anything you do not want to see or hear. He will not try to change your behavior, your mind about an issue, or be passive-aggressive when he can't get his way.

I grew up witnessing the toxic relationship of my parents. It was an extremely abusive situation and tainted my view of relationships in general. I worked very hard at protecting my emotions and avoiding meaningful relationships, as I never wanted to be a victim as my mother was. In a sense, that was an unhealthy method of coping, but I viewed it as a survival technique. I quickly observed the clichéd men who were just like my father, and purposefully avoided them so as not to be a statistic. I met my current husband in college and he was the complete opposite of everything my father was. We became friends first but had a strong attraction that couldn't be avoided. We've been married 10 years now and have 2 children together. We've had our ups and downs as in all relationships, but we have a very strong communication base and are committed to our marriage. We trust each other and value each other's love and friendship.

Stephania Vereen - Author, Speaker, Blogger
www.stephaniavereen.com

Spiritual

This may seem like an odd characteristic to throw into the mix, but the truth is, spirituality is foundational to a great relationship. This is the core of a person's moral code and values. This is where the golden rule is formed and grows. Don't get me wrong though, being spiritual does not mean you are religious. There is a big difference. In fact, religion has been at the center of many crummy marriages and relationships but that is a topic for another book.

A spiritual man understands the mind, body, soul connection. He is aware and acknowledges there is something greater than he is. He understands his strength is derived from a source outside of himself but is learning how to tap into that source and become the best person he can be. A spiritual man respects and grows to love humanity and the earth. He knows he was given the responsibility to care for both as he cares for himself.

A spiritual man will treat the woman in his life with kindness and see her as a fellow traveler in this world. He is able to tap into the energy that connects all humanity and be a part of all things good.

A man who is spiritual is not perfect but embraces his imperfection and finds it in his heart to accept the imperfections in others. He is learning to live by the law of love instead of fear. His actions are dictated by this law so he treats the woman he is dating or mated to with love and respect.

Well, what about church you say. My answer is the man you encounter may or may not go to church. He may be heavily involved in some kind of ministry or he may give his time and resources to charity. He may spend time reading the Bible or some other religious book. He may run or help a youth mentoring program or he may volunteer at a nursing home. These activities are just an outgrowth of his heart. You will know if he is trying to punch a ticket or get some kind of credit for his actions beyond just doing it for the sake of humanity.

When you have a truly spiritual man or at least one who is striving to be one, you have a good thing. His heart is in the right place and his heart will be for you.

Integrity

Integrity is defined as "the quality of being honest and having strong moral principles; moral uprightness." You can count on a man of integrity to be honest at all times. This honesty will spread across every aspect of his life. He will not just be honest with you but with everyone and in every situation he encounters.

Seems like a pretty high standard because everyone tells white lies or perhaps steals pens from the company supply closet, right? To be a man of integrity is to maintain a sense of right and wrong under all circumstances. It doesn't mean they are infallible. It means they do not make a habit of lying and stealing as a way of life.

With a man of integrity you can feel secure in the knowledge he will never put your lives in jeopardy because of illegal activities, financial mismanagement, or anything that would cause him or you to be put in harm's way.

Above all, you will not have to worry about him lying to you. A man of integrity will tell you the truth about everything. Sometimes it will feel like he tells you too much, but know this is a good thing. You will be able to trust his word, but more importantly you will come to depend on his honesty in word and deed.

Beware of the man who lies to himself. It may seem odd to put the previous sentence here but it is an important sentence. Why? Because a man who lies to himself about his state of mind, his behavior, or his past will lie to you. A man in denial can only do harm to himself and your relationship.

The Perfect Man?

It seems like I've described the perfect man. I suppose I have to a degree, but what I've described is a model of the kind of man you will want to seek. It is a baseline of behavior to expect if you want a healthy relationship. No man is perfect and the man you are dating may not have all these qualities, yet. Notice the word "yet." But every man has it in himself to develop those qualities.

You have the power to bring it out through your behavior, your standards, and your encouragement. Notice I didn't say you should bring it out through coaxing, manipulation, or outright boot camp-style behavior. He will never respond to that, but he will respond to positive reinforcement, your standards, and your encouragement. It is up to you to learn how to use your power for good so you have the relationship you want.

As an African-American woman, I began to lose hope in finding a man who could be my equal partner in life. I dated some men who definitely weren't as put together as I would have liked. Some of the men I dated had no college degree, children, and living with their parents, etc., while I was a resident physician, living on my own, working and supporting myself while completing my specialty training.

Then I met a man who took my breath away. We clicked immediately, had great conversation, he was smart, had his own business and we seemed to have a lot in common. He did have children, but he was supporting them and I figured I could give the relationship a shot. There was a significant age difference, 8 years, but this wasn't the nail in the coffin.

Three years of trying to prove myself to him, show him that I was capable of settling down and that I would be a good mate. I never met his family, his children or any of his friends. He tired easily hearing about my work and my life, the things that were important to me.

In the end it was my brother who made me realize that things in this relationship had gone terribly awry. He told me, "You have to realize when a relationship has become toxic, and get out." Thankfully, that relationship ended and I have since found my life partner. He is wonderful, emotionally available, a great support, a great love and a great friend. We are getting married in 8 months!

Cherise H.

Samantha A. Gregory

13 TAPPING INTO YOUR POWER AS A WOMAN

What does that mean really to tap into your power as a woman? How do you do that? What power do women have? It took me a while to understand that I had power even though one of my biggest male fans told me that I had it over and over again. I think I was afraid of that power or didn't really believe it was real. But as time has gone on and I've had more life experiences than I care to recount, I've learned that I truly have power.

All women have power. Why do you think there has been such a concerted effort to suppress women? Why do you think that men, since the dawn of time, have done everything in their power to make women feel weak and inadequate and completely dependent on them? What secret are they trying their best to keep us from finding out? They know how much power we have because our power affects them. Our power makes them feel week and hopelessly bound by our presence.

Though we have this power, it is not to be used for evil.

Unfortunately, a few women grew drunk on this power and damaged a lot of men. In return these men have done everything in their power to stifle every woman they meet. Whether it is political power, religious power, or emotional power, many men have used these elements to turn the tables and keep women blinded to their true potential.

Despite a few rouge females, the power of women still remains a mystery to most and a source of fear to others. The question that looms in your mind is likely, what is this power and how do I tap into it?

The power of a woman is her essence, her physical beauty, her inner steadiness and charm. Because men are visual creatures they are automatically a slave to the physical form of a woman. They lose all mental faculties in the presence of a beautiful woman. Their mouth goes dry and their tongue swells up so they can't speak. For a split second, they lose consciousness because you walked into the room.

You might think this can't possibly be true because no man you know does that. Perhaps you can't see it, but there is at least one man who gets weak in the knees over you. If it's not happening take a good look in the mirror after you finish reading this chapter to find out what's going on. The effect you have on a man should be memorable.

Your capacity to love, heal and nurture is captivating and powerful. Think of the power a mother has over her son. She is the first woman he typically falls in love with and the one who has the most influence over him. She can make or break his life and affects all of his relationships. Mothers and women in general are guiding beacons in the life of every man.

A woman who is self-possessed, self-loving, kind, and beautiful on the inside and the outside is a force to be reckoned with. She holds unlimited power in her hands to lift up or tear down an entire generation of men.

Taking hold of that power is your right. Using it in a way that will uplift and empower others is your responsibility. With the power to change a man's life, you could change the course of history.

So how do you use this power? How do you tap into it so you live your best life and bring out the best in others? The first thing to do is recognize that you are powerful and can bring joy, goodness and peace into the life of the man you've chosen to be with.

You can use your power to receive the

- Time
- Attention
- Support
- Exclusivity
- Respect
- Honesty
- ...and Love you deserve!

Learning how to speak so you get what you need as well as use body language to elicit the kind of response and action you desire is an art. There are many books on the subject, but I would like to share the basic ingredients for getting all you want and deserve.

Use very few words

Men can't process all the words we want to say to them. We may have a great argument, story, or vent, but they just cannot hold all that information in one setting. They will zone out and will not be able to repeat what we have said. They will not be able to answer all of our ten questions and you will feel like they are not listening to you. To solve this problem learn to speak in sound bites. Discuss one issue at a time. Ask one question at a time. Request one thing at a time.

Drop unresolved issues quickly

Ladies, we tend to nag. We become like the dripping faucet the Psalmist described in the Bible. We can go on and on about an issue until we drive the man we have chosen to be with away. If you keep in mind that he wants to make you happy and he has the best intentions, you will not fall into the trap of thinking he doesn't care about your feelings. You will keep yourself from stress and anxiety because you believe he never listens to you. The truth is men have a running list of priorities. If what you are requesting is not high on that list, it will not get done right away.

I've been told they weigh your request against the other things on their mental list and if does not directly benefit them, well... it gets shelved until they have time or inclination to do it. I know he used to do everything you wanted when you first started dating or early in your marriage. That is because he was getting a direct benefit.

He was going to get your smile and nod of approval. He was going to get something that made him feel good; he was going to get you. But time and experience wears away these feelings of being rewarded. Maybe you've stopped smiling or giving nods of approval. Maybe you started making him feel obligated to do what you want him to do. He gets no reward in that and I'm sorry to burst your bubble, but love has little to do with it in his mind. Sure he loves you, but he is not motivated by that emotion when it comes to doing tasks for you. He is motivated by rewards. Which leads into the next ingredient for using your power. Action.

Take action

Action can mean several things. It could mean you take a sledge hammer to his game console or it could mean you give him the stare of a thousand daggers. Whatever action means to you, use it to motivate him to action. I heard a few years ago that men don't hear but they feel. How true that statement is. It took me a while to understand that, but when I did it made my life so much easier. When I took action I had to use fewer words and didn't get myself all worked up over things where men were concerned.

My action could be direct or it could be subtle. It all depended on the man I was dealing with. Sometimes the action would be an unpleasant experience for him and at other times it would be like a kid in a candy store. The action you choose to take will be up to you to decide.

What I can share is you should not be above misplacing the remote control, burning the dinner a few nights in a row, turning his underwear pink, or any number of other subtle messages to get his attention. In the same way, you should not be above giving him a neck rub, bringing his plate, putting the kids to bed early, or any other positive reinforcements.

Actions always speak louder than words. They make the

world go 'round and they get you the results you want. Action is all a part of tapping into your power and inner wisdom as a woman. Pain and pleasure are yours to give. Of course you would rather give pleasure, but sometimes pain must be the tool of choice.

Smile no matter what

Seems fake to do this but trust me, you attract more bees to honey than to vinegar. Now is not the time to flex your feminist muscles. Use your feminine charms to get what you want.

Many men have told me that if the women in their lives would speak in a sweet voice and call them "Big Daddy" (or their preferred terms of endearment) they would give them anything they wanted. They don't mind if you exploit their tender spot. They want you to because it makes them feel important and needed.

When you ask for what you want with a smile you get what you want about 90% of the time. Even if what you have to say is not pleasant, when you say it with a smile it softens the blow. If you are refusing to do something you can say it with a smile. You can phase anything so it makes the man in your life feel validated and respected. That is all he wants from you. You have the power to make things happen in your relationship.

Take the seat of relationship power

Let's face it; men are clueless when it comes to managing relationships. Why do you think they let you make all the decisions? They don't know what to do and they are afraid they will screw it up. They just want to make you happy. So if you have to decide where you will go out to eat, be happy you get to choose. If you want him to choose, make a list of your favorite places and email it to him. It makes it easier for him to choose a place you will enjoy.

Don't be offended if he doesn't think about taking you to romantic picnics or the summer festival. You have to suggest it and let him make the final decision, which is usually yes. You have to tell him your favorite flower if you want them. You have to tell him the kind of movies, food, candy, and perfume you like. Make him the hero and the mastermind even though you are the one influencing his choices. He doesn't mind and will be relieved.

Sometimes we expect too much from the men in our lives. We expect him to read our minds then we get angry when he doesn't do what we want him to do. We set him and ourselves up for failure and it's not fair. So do yourself a favor and take the reins of the relationship. He will thank you and you will be much happier. You are the Queen of Hearts, not in a murderous way, but from an emotional and relational standpoint. He can't be that in the relationship so let him off the hook. Talk in sound bites to find out if he is okay with you taking control of this part of the relationship. At another time, share what you like. In another sound bite, share what you'd like to do.

These are a few basics to tapping into your power as a woman. You can go deeper in other books that I will recommend later. In the meantime, use your power for good and get the cake you deserve!

He was unemployed for the 15 years our marriage lasted, so I had to work full time to support our three children and us. Projecting his faults onto me regularly while never questioning his own behavior, he would taunt me with words like parasite, mental retard, fat, deformed, idiot, etc. I can still see the look of contempt on his face as our marriage continued and I tried desperately to save it.

We tried a marriage course at my church — he went once and refused to return. We went to see a counselor — he concluded it was a waste of time and never went back. Needless to say, I had to pay for all this. He only brought fines and massive debts home which he got me to pay by being kind for a few days or more usually, blackmailing me with things to do with the children. Unfortunately, my self-esteem had sunk so low by the time the abuse was at its worse. I thought he was right and I deserved no better. I dreaded going out with him because inevitably when we left any company he would fly into a violent temper over something I had done or said, or failed to do, or worn, or whatever, comparing me unfavorably with all the other women.

Elaine Purnell
Author of The Mistress

14 DATING PRIMER

By now you are living your life for cake and not crumbs. You are ready to go into new dating experiences with a different perspective. You've probably changed in a way that has caused the man in your life to exit stage left to your joy and relief. Crumb droppers usually don't stay around because it does not benefit them. You are better off and can now be open to new experiences. This time around you will be prepared and open to a wonderful dating experience. Above all you will have fun in the process.

Dating can be frustrating and scary because you have expectations. There is frustration about how you look, whether you will say the right thing, wondering if he thinks you are acceptable, and so on. You can drive yourself crazy with all the chatter going on in your head. The first thing to do is calm down and breath. You will be okay. You will not fall flat on your face with the proper preparation. This can be a fun experience. You just have to find your bliss and your sweet spot. This primer will show you how.

Find your bliss

When you find your bliss, you are in the right frame of mind and have the right perspective to begin dating for cake. What is bliss? It's that place of absolute joy and peace with yourself. It's self-love and acceptance. It's that feeling that nothing can go wrong in your life because all the pieces to the puzzle are in place for you, or at least on the table ready to be put together.

When you find your bliss you will be relaxed and waiting with anticipation for good things to happen in your life. To do this you have to let go of expectations you have been holding on to. You have to release the hurt, baggage, and anger that may have been plaguing your life. You have to forgive yourself for letting others hurt and control you. You have to forgive yourself for all the perceived failures and embrace yourself.

You have to know you are lovable, acceptable, and enough. It may feel like you are none of those things, but the truth is you are. We talked about your worth and value in previous chapters. This is the same thing. You are all that because you were created to be a shining star in this world. There is no one like you; there never has been and never will be anyone else like you. You have the power to live up to your fullest potential. You have to power to love all that you are so make a vow to treat yourself better and let yourself off the hook. You do not have to be perfect. As I like to say, "I'm perfectly imperfect and I like me just the way I am!" I encourage you to take this affirmation as your own. Become your own best friend and give yourself a break. When you do that you begin to see glimpses of your true self emerging and the bliss follows close behind this realization of your awesomeness!

Get over yourself

This sounds harsh. I just talked about loving and accepting yourself. I just told you to be kind to yourself and become your own best friend and here I go telling you to get over yourself. Feels like a contradiction doesn't it? Let me explain it like this.

Too many times we get in our own way. We let our feelings of inadequacy and feelings of not being enough cloud our judgment. We think everyone thinks the way we do about who we are. Ironically, this is true. People do feel the way you feel about yourself. It is how we teach people to treat us. So if you think you are ugly, undesirable, and can't possibly be attractive that is what other people will think too. You emit positive and negative energy. People, especially men, pick up on this energy and will react to you based on the energy you are putting off. If you have been putting off negative energy because you feel unsure, unsafe, and unworthy, the people you encounter will assume you are.

They will either keep you at a distance or they will use your insecurities to their advantage. You will end up with crumbs or with nothing at all. Now is the time to get over yourself. This is especially true if you feel shy, timid, anxious, and nervous about dating and meeting new people. Getting over yourself means you stop thinking about all the things that is wrong with you and all the things that inhibit you. Maybe you feel fat, pimply faced, and frumpy. Maybe you think your voice is too squeaky or too deep. Maybe you think your hands or feet are too big. Maybe you think your hair is too blah or that nothing about you is sexy.

If you think those things you can be sure others will think it if you point it out. Otherwise, they probably don't notice. If you feel bad about these things you have the power to change it. You can get a makeover. You can do something about it.

Despite all the things that are wrong with you, there are many more things that are right about you. You just have to choose to see them. Make a list of your best features, qualities, and accomplishments then promise to think about only those things for the next 10 days. You will feel differently and can finally get over yourself.

When you get over yourself you will be more concerned about shining your light into the world. You will not think about your flaws but your fabulousness. You will want to share it with the world. Your concern will be about spreading your positive energy to everyone you meet. As a result, you will become a magnet for positive people and experiences.

Open Your Heart

When you find your bliss and get over yourself you will be filled with positive energy. But that might not be preparation enough to begin a new journey into the dating world. You may still have a few apprehensions about letting someone new into your life. There may be a little bruising here and there around your heart. There may be a little pain (or a lot) and you may feel gun shy. The best course of action is to feel the full range of feelings then release them.

Choose the Right Dating Channels

Before you start dating as the new you, decide what the purpose of it will be. Do you want to meet a lot of great guys? Do you want to meet the "one"? Do you want to find a boyfriend or a future husband? What is your motive going in to the dating world? Your motive will determine which dating channels to use.

If you are looking for a casual dating experience then you could check out the personals on Craigslist or free casual dating sites like Skout or Datehookup. The people on these sites are looking for fun and a fling. You might be able to find a few diamonds in the rough but most people on those sites are not looking for a long-term relationship or love.

To meet a higher quality man you will do better to get yourself on a paid dating site like eHarmony or Match.com. The people on those sites are ready for a serious relationship and are looking for the "one" 9 times out of 10.

If you are ready for a match made in heaven and are really serious about finding a husband you will do best to get the help of a matchmaker or enlist the help of family and friends who want to see you happy and have a wide circle of friends.

Most importantly, as I mentioned before, you must be ready for love and ready to meet the man of your dreams. This means you have an open heart and mind and trust that love will find you.

You must also hold back judgment and faultfinding when you meet new men. If you have ever experienced dating a man that always talked about his ex and how she wronged him, you know what a turn off it is to listen to that kind of whining. Maybe you've dated men who always found fault in every woman he's dated, his mother, and every woman on the planet. Again, it's a turn off. Steer clear of these kinds of men and do not become that kind of woman.

I think that if I choose to talk about my toxic relationship it will take more then 2-3 paragraphs, lol. So I prefer talking about my new and healthy relationship that I have ever had since I started dating. The steps that I have chosen to take this time around is that I laid down on paper exactly what I wanted for my love life, and I stick to it, even if that means staying single for years!!! And through prayer and a positive outlook on my life and myself, I am sure that I have found the ONE. Even if it does not work out (but for now I refuse to think negatively) I know exactly where I want to go, and I am sure that I will find it with the help of GOD. Here is my list: A GOD FEARING MAN, A FINANCIALLY STABLE MAN, A FAMILY MAN MEANING HE ALREADY HAS KIDS and knows what living together means, and A RESPECTFUL MAN (he respect himself first, so automatically he will respect me).

G.B.

---

15 GO GET YOUR CAKE

We hear all the time that relationships are hard or tough. They make us crazy sometimes and can fill us with either extreme joy or extreme anxiety. Sometimes we choose the wrong people and it feels like a lifetime of pain we endure. Then something happens and we say enough; we get out and save ourselves for someone better. Ironically, that rarely happens until we become someone "better."

The journey to a No More Crumbs Dating and Mating life will not be easy unless you have already done the work required to move toward healthy relationships. It is a process and must be embarked upon like a great voyage. Trust me, at the end of the process, you will feel lighter, worthy, and able to say no to the crumbs and yes to the cake!

The power is in your hands if you will just recognize that you are the prize. Keep in mind that the journey is not about becoming perfect, but about releasing the chains of the past, all the unhealthy relationships and associated memories that keep you from making healthy choices. Only a healthy mind and soul makes healthy decisions.

Even as I continue journeying through life, I find I have to go through a process or two to shake off the crumbs that still linger in my life. Just when I thought I was done, another issue surfaces. I'm learning not to be upset with myself when I hit a wall. It's life. It happens and I can get through it because I've been through far worse.

The point is we are all in different places and spaces in our lives. I may be a little further along than you, but that doesn't make me better. It just makes me a little wiser because of my experiences.

So I'll leave you with two lists. They are meant to encourage and motivate you to begin living an exceptional life. They are meant to help you move from crumbs to cake in dating/mating to a yummy cake-filled life. List one is my Guidelines for Living and list two is the No More Crumbs Woman Mantra.

Guidelines for Living Loved: The No More Crumbs Woman Rules

Rule #1 – Love Yourself

Rule #2 – Take Your Time

Rule #3 – Say Yes to Your Brilliance

Rule #4 – Trust Your Intuition

Rule #5 – Never Accept Second Place or Second Best

Rule #6 – Expect Excellence

Rule #7 – Be Graceful

Rule #8 – Be a Lady

Rule #9 – Recognize Your Worth

Rule #10 – Embrace Your Power

No More Crumbs Woman Mantra

In an exclusive relationship
you deserve his:

- Time
- Attention
- Support
- Exclusivity
- Respect
- Honesty
- ... and Love!

ABOUT THE AUTHOR

Samantha Gregory writes, parents, and lives with joy and passion. She shares wisdom gathered from years of experiences that taught her about life, love, and freedom.

She is the author of *100 Secrets of Successful Single Motherhood*, *The Single Mom Grant Guide*, and several other books. She blogs at RichSingleMomma.com, is a freelance writer, and a tireless renaissance woman. She is also an oddly happy introvert, creative spirit, and lover of books and music.

She is the CIO (Chief Inspiration Officer) of No More Crumbs Women's Empowerment Initiative. She sets out to encourage, empower and help women in toxic relationships recognize their worth, embrace their freedom, and attract love (and wealth).

She lives in the Metro Atlanta area with her two children.